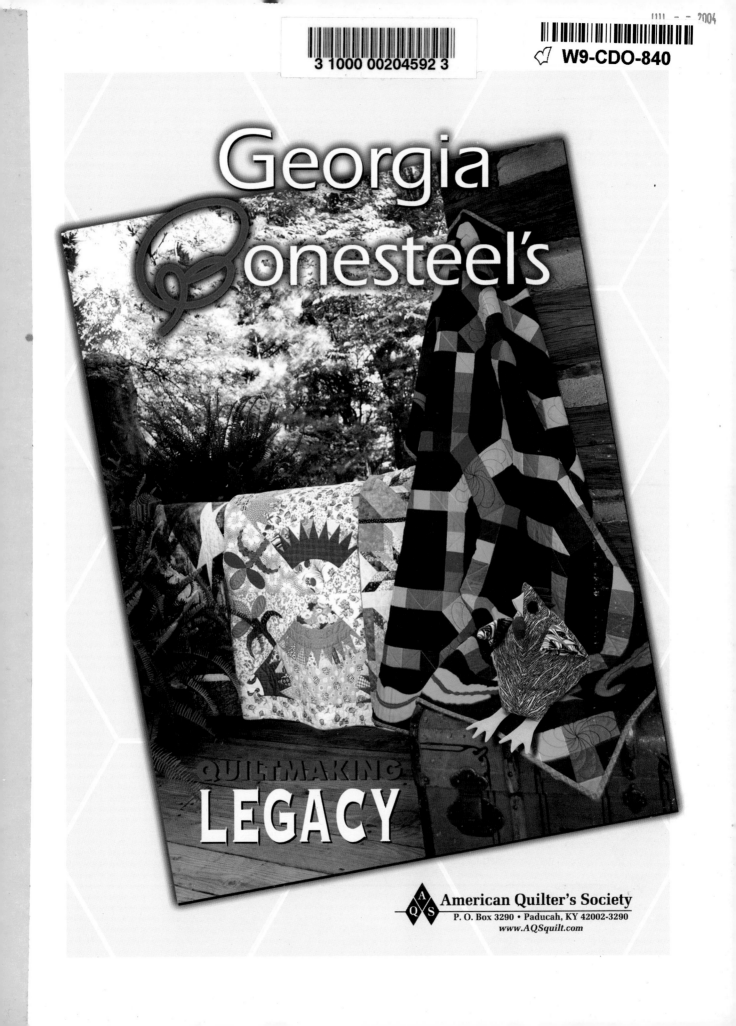

# Georgia Bonesteel's

## QUILTMAKING LEGACY

American Quilter's Society
P. O. Box 3290 • Paducah, KY 42002-3290
www.AQSquilt.com

Located in Paducah, Kentucky, the American Quilter's Society (AQS) is dedicated to promoting the accomplishments of today's quilters. Through its publications and events, AQS strives to honor today's quiltmakers and their work and to inspire future creativity and innovation in quiltmaking.

EDITOR: BARBARA SMITH

GRAPHIC DESIGN: ELAINE WILSON

COVER DESIGN: MICHAEL BUCKINGHAM

PHOTOGRAPHY: CHARLES R. LYNCH, UNLESS OTHERWISE NOTED

ILLUSTRATIONS: SAMUEL BALDWIN

**Library of Congress Cataloging-in-Publication Data**

Bonesteel, Georgia.

   Georgia Bonesteel's quiltmaking legacy / by Georgia Bonesteel

   p. cm.

ISBN 1-57432-844-1

  1. Patchwork--Patterns. 2. Quilting. 3. Quilted goods. 4. Quilts. I. Title: Quiltmaking legacy. II. Title.

   TT835.B5788   2004

   746.46--dc22

                            2004001159

Additional copies of this book may be ordered from the American Quilter's Society, PO Box 3290, Paducah, KY 42002-3290; 800-626-5420 (orders only please); or online at www.AQSquilt.com. For all other inquiries, call 270-898-7903.

# Dedication

*To our grandchildren: Jinkinson, Georgia, Ellery, Anna, Claire, Jane, and Jonah. (Maggie, we remember.)*

*May they find a passion.*

PHOTO: LOGAN PHOTOGRAPHICS

Posies 'Round The Pickle Dish. Project begins on page 125.

# Contents

# Introduction

If my stitches could talk, what a tale they would weave. In fact, my patchwork life is similar to woven cloth. The lengthwise warp yarns are those first applied to the loom and they are the strongest. These are my parents, my husband, my children, my sister, and now my grandchildren, forming stability over a 30-year span of quiltmaking. The woof, or crosswise yarns, form character and create the "zip" to make the fabric beautiful. These are my students, fellow professionals, a myriad of quilt patterns, the sewing machine I depend on and, of course, fabric. Genetics and a strong work ethic imparted by high-achieving parents, along with an endless appreciation of color, woven into the fabric, hold it all together.

Welcome to my quilt world. This book tells my story. I have no secrets. Quilts have a way of revealing all, and inside all my stitches is the tale of how I got started, my motives, my mentors, and my current results. Along this path have been many friends and fellow teachers. Early in my quilt life, I tried to imagine all of my fellow travelers living on a street, each of us in a home depicted by our specialty. I evolved this concept into a quilt series called "The Street Where We Live." A few professional quilters' homes from my past are shown in the patchwork banners on the bottom of pages 6–9. One special gentleman, Toni DeChesere, has passed on, but left his drafting mark in our world.

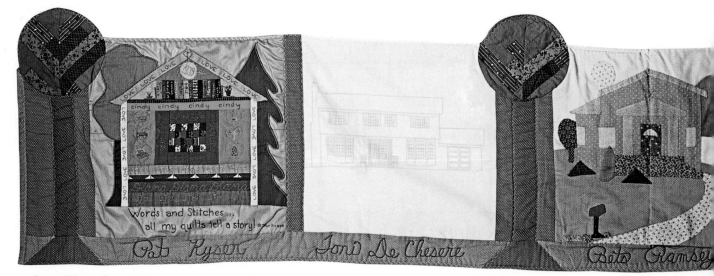

STREET WHERE QUILTERS LIVE

Road blocks or quilt detours are also a part of the street where we live. I'm not talking about design problems or searching for that perfect fabric solution. I'm talking about physical setbacks that aren't exactly planned. In my case, it was an acoustic neuroma, a non-cancerous brain tumor near my right eardrum.

In the fall of 1985, I was involved with classes in Houston, Texas, for the International Quilt Association, and I had two other major quilt projects scheduled for the following year: my fourth book and the taping of my fifth *Lap Quilting* television series. After a routine dentist visit, there was a numbness around my mouth, so I assumed there was a damaged nerve. Everything checked out at the dentist, so he sent me to my regular doctor. After a cortisone dose pack, things got worse in that I was having trouble swallowing. Then there was that fateful day – I walked my four miles in the morning, then went for a cat scan. That evening my doctor phoned and said he wanted to come see me at home, with my husband present. How many times does your doctor make a house call? My husband was deer hunting, so my neighbor and longtime secretary, Norma, came to hold my hand. The diagnosis was a brain tumor. The shock was overwhelming because I really felt in good health.

Within the week, I was in the hospital. Ever the quilter, I took a quilt with me. It was my entry into the Statue of Liberty contest, and there was a deadline! The surgery was seven hours. I still remember calling a recovery room nurse an angel because, after such surgery, you are happy just to be alive.

Afterward, I was desperate to talk to anyone who had had a brain tumor. There were so many questions to ask and so much to understand about the changes that occurred. I lost the hearing in my right ear, but that was not as bad as not being able to really smile. Three major nerves on the right side of my face were left with permanent damage. I could still quilt, but how could I ever be on television again?

Boxes of get-well cards from quilters all over this country were sent to me at the hospital. At one point, a nurse asked me, "Just who are you?" It took six months for my sagging face to come back and my right eye to open and close naturally. During that time, family and the support of friends made all the difference.

Flavin Glover          Jean Ray Laury          Yvonne Porcella

STREET WHERE QUILTERS LIVE

Fortunately, I discovered a support network, the Acoustic Neuroma Association. ANA is a wonderful association that updates the current medical breakthroughs for these tumors and answers many questions for patients. What I took away from the experience was much more than the physical changes. Quilting, writing books, and teaching, including television appearances, certainly had a higher priority than having a crooked smile. It is one's heart and one's will to go forward that really matters.

ANA, 600 PEACHTREE PARKWAY, SUITE #108, CUMMING, GA 30041; WWW.ANAUSA.ORG

## What can you find in this book?

The many requests for my now vintage crazy-patch handbags have been fulfilled with two styles presented: the envelope-style and the box-style (pages 15–20).

Sampler quilts have been my mainstay over the years. We have come a long way when almost the entire sampler, in three block sizes, can be cut out with simple measurements and

STREET WHERE QUILTERS LIVE

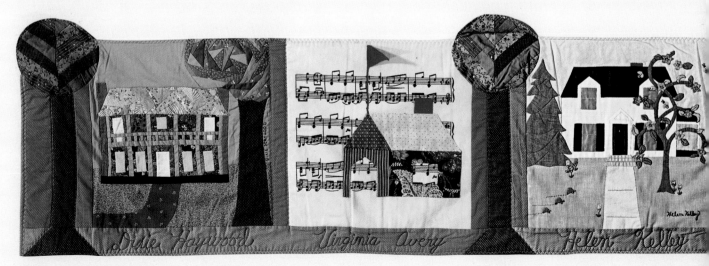

STREET WHERE QUILTERS LIVE

a rotary cutter. Three of the blocks in the TEACHING SAMPLER (page 21) will need templates, however: Crazy Patch, Dresden Plate, and Grandmother's Fan.

Making mountain quilts is a natural reflection of my home scene here in North Carolina (MANY MOUNTAINS VARIATION, page 64), and what better way to celebrate grandchildren than with "patch-fun" garments (Get-Real Garments, page 67).

Is it possible to escape for a week of quiltmaking combined with fun times? See the proof with the Freedom Escape quilts (page 90). For those who want the novelty, quick fix for patchwork, there are many options in the chapter Just Got to Make (page 133).

The quilts I made have become a journal filled with stories and corrections. I have made my share of mistakes, always knowing that even a mistake is something to pass on to students. Maybe that is why we keep making quilts – to finally get it right. These become the blue ribbon winners at quilt shows and the coveted quilts that form our legacy. So get ready – replace your rotary cutter blade, restack your stash, and put a new needle in your sewing machine.

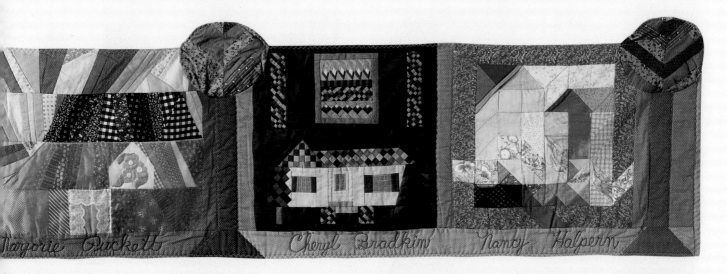

# Chapter 1

# Once Upon a Time

So often I am reminded of how I got here from there. The trigger might be a scrap of fabric, a newspaper interview, or just organizing a quilt fabric stash. Sewing has always been a part of my lifestyle. Even when I was a little girl, my mother put a needle and thread in my hand. With my extra energy, she discovered that sewing kept me out of trouble and easily occupied.

My first project was hexagons. It did not take long to discover that I could only set those obtuse angles together by leaving loose seam allowances – lesson number one – free floating seam intersections. How ironic to realize, years later, that the first full-sized top I quilted (on a wobbly standing frame) was a Grandmother's Flower Garden. It had been made by my great grandmother, Charlotte Bradshaw Sayler, from Portage, Ohio. Then, coming full circle, another hexagon design created from a set of plastic puzzle blocks by our granddaughter, Little Georgia, was made into a wallhanging.

**ABOVE:** Georgia's first project as a child, age 9.
**ABOVE RIGHT:** LOTTIE'S GRANDMOTHER'S FLOWER GARDEN QUILT. Grandmother's Flower Garden quilt made by Georgia's great grandmother, Charlotte Bradshaw Sayler, Portage, Ohio. PHOTO: GEORGIA BONESTEEL

**ABOVE:** Georgia's granddaughter, Little Georgia, enjoys a hexagon puzzle.

**RIGHT:** HANDS ALL AROUND wallhanging, made by the author from Little Georgia's hexagon puzzle design.

From making doll clothes to being a clothing and textiles major in college, I find that fabric and stitching have played a major role in my life. It was not until, as a family of five, we moved to New Orleans, that I had a chance to exploit my dressmaking skills. It was not exactly a couture experience on a French runway, but I did make a winning ensemble from a Vogue pattern. I even modeled it at a major department store on Canal Street. This led to an audition as a seamstress for a sewing machine company's how-to television show. Fortunately, I won the audition.

With the children in school, there was more time for sewing. I discovered a pattern for making neckties, which meant that my husband, Pete, was wearing the latest polyester and the widest homemade ties to work. The leftovers from the bias-made ties led to another opportunity – patchwork pillows. So when the *Sewing Is Fun* crew needed a topic for another show, my patchwork career on TV was launched.

With boxes of leftover scrap fabric from a major necktie company, I tried various forms of patchwork, from string piecing and sew-and-flip to small traditional blocks, using these lovely tie silks. My results were pretty, but limp and without body until I added batting between the layers. Finally there was enough stability to make one-of-a-kind purses. My patchwork pillows evolved into small evening bags for a cottage industry called "Cajun Quilters." Why, I even had a one-room store, for about a week, next to Pat O'Briens in the French Quarter. The first handbag I sold came back the next day. There were pins left inside where I had neglected to secure the lining! It was so much fun to make something for resale as I provided inventory for these unique boutiques. During this time, I sometimes rode my bicycle from the west bank along the levee, across the Mississippi River on a ferry, and into the French Quarter.

A move to North Carolina led me to traditional quilts. A neighbor on our new street was looking for someone to take her teaching job as a sewing instructor at the Blue Ridge Community College. I lucked into the job immediately. However, patchwork had become my "thing," so I soon switched courses.

After I introduced patchwork for the adult education courses, my in-depth research began. It consisted of trips to the library and quilting with a group of ladies at a local retirement organization, called The Opportunity House. There I struggled with an old-fashioned quilting frame. I was the young "whippersnapper," the odd-ball at the frame, so it was not unusual for them to request, "Please, Georgia, make smaller stitches!" I was also naive enough to think that the students in my classes would quilt on each other's quilts to complete them. That did not work, but if they quilted on smaller sections, they could be successful. Lap Quilting was born!

**ABOVE:** Georgia with some of her one-of-a-kind purses.
**TOP LEFT:** Cajun Quilters sign from Georgia's one-room store in the French Quarter in New Orleans.
**BOTTOM LEFT:** To fit the time restrictions of a class, students quilted on smaller sections … the beginning of lap quilting. Blocks by Mary Ruth Branyon. PHOTOS: GEORGIA BONESTEEL

In 1975, my mother saw a knitting show on television and immediately thought, why not an instructional quilting show? So with a carload of quilts and an outline, I approached the University of North Carolina public television station in Chapel Hill. By 1978, we had taped the very first how-to quilting show for television. I taught just as I did in class, only this time I had to imagine 25 eager students in one little "hole." The lesson plan was a sampler, just like my beginning quilt classes. Back then, we used cardboard templates and carefully drew around each one before cutting the fabric pieces out with scissors. My, have we come a long way!

For my 1100 series on public television, I once again turned to a sampler. I have always been drawn to sampler quilts. After all, you must crawl before you walk. In the COUNTRY TO COUNTRY SAMPLER, page 32, 6" blocks float around a center print panel, alive with color. Any favorite print fabric could set the style for this sampler. Each block depicts a show theme for the 13-week series, but you can experiment with this setting for any of your favorite 6" blocks. Keep a folder or picture book of all the various sampler settings, and before you know it, you will be teaching that sampler class and passing on your heritage.

## Crazy Patch My Way

I really owe my quilting career to crazy patch. The askew angles and the balance of print fabrics versus textured velvets and silks, along with the fancy embroidery stitches, became the foundation for my small evening bags. I started making these more than 30 years ago. I developed two crazy-patch methods for small evening bags and for garments, such as vests and jackets. The first method is called "predictable patchwork." For this method, an iron-on paper with a ¼" grid (Grid Grip™), is used to make templates. In the second method, called "unpredictable patchwork," the fabric pieces are sewn on a cloth foundation.

Here is an opportunity for you to select a varied mixture of fabrics, from corduroy to velvet to suede, along with silk and rayon. If you are using old, worn neckties, do wash them first. Then gently take them apart, removing the interfacing or lining, so they will lie flat. Any ties that fall apart in the laundry should be eliminated. To stabilize silks or rayons, a lightweight fusible can be pressed on the back. I prefer the knit fusible.

Read through the following instructions and select the style of handbag you want to make, either envelope or box, and the type of crazy patch, planned or unplanned.

## Planned Patchwork

**1.** For the envelope style, cut a piece of iron-on grid paper 10" x 23". For the box style, cut three grid-paper sections: two 7" squares and one 7" x 8½" rectangle.

**2.** To create crazy-patch templates, use a ruler and pencil to draw random lines at odd angles on the grid paper. Keep in mind the size of each template in relation to the next one as you draw. Code the templates according to the order in which they will be stitched together (fig. 1–1, page 14).

*Please note that the grid-paper image will be the reverse of the finished piece because the templates are pressed on the backs of the fabrics.*

**3.** Cut the coded templates apart. Place each template on the back of your selected fabric, aligning the grid with the fabric's grain line. Press the templates on the fabrics with an iron on the cotton setting. Use a rotary cutter and ruler to trim away excess fabric, leaving a ¼" seam allowance around all sides.

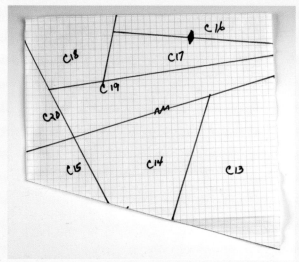

**Fig. 1–1.** Templates drawn on grid paper, with coding.

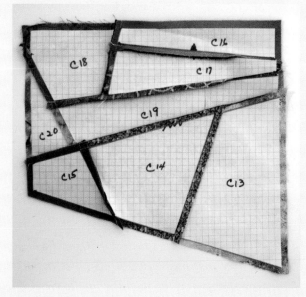

**Fig. 1–2.** Cut-apart templates, pressed and sewn together.

**4.** Taking the pieces in order, match the grid lines and the paper edges. "Pin and peek" for accurate stitching. Once pinned in place, the template on the bottom can be removed, leaving the top one for a stitching guide. Machine sew the pieces together, then remove all the paper templates (fig. 1–2).

Templates can be reused many times. Store them in a well-marked envelope or press them onto fabric.

## Unplanned Patchwork

**1.** Cut a cloth foundation for either the envelope style (10½" x 23½") or the box style (two 7½" squares and one 7½" x 9" rectangle). Select random fabrics and cut them into odd shapes that are similar in size.

*You will need about 20 shapes for each style of handbag. Balance the prints, solids, colors, weaving, and textures of the fabrics for a unique style. Sometimes one print can be the springboard for a theme.*

**2.** Pin a fabric shape, wrong side down, on the foundation, either in the center or a corner. Pick up a second fabric piece and align the raw edges of the two fabrics, right sides together, for the first seam. Sew through the foundation and flip the top piece up. Pin each successive shape in place as you cover the foundation.

*Sometimes, if you like, you can pre-stitch the pieces together before adding them to the foundation. Any unusual fabrics can be hand appliquéd.*

**3.** Once the foundation is covered, trim the envelope-style rectangle to 10" x 23". Trim the two box-style squares to 7" and the one rectangle to 7" x 8½".

# Crazy-Patch Handbags
*Envelope-Style*
*and*
*Box-Style*

## MATERIALS

Planned or unplanned crazy-patch rectangle 10" x 23"

Batting, backing, and lining, each cut 10" x 23"

Novelty button and shoulder chain, 33" to 35" long

Bias-cut piece of fabric for loops, 1" x 6"

Embroidery thread, black or colors to match crazy patch

## Assembly

**1.** Stack the crazy patch, batting, and backing pieces and baste them together. Stitching through all three layers, cover the pieced seams with embroidery stitches by hand, machine, or a combination of both.

*Use your machine novelty stitches and be creative by embroidering areas of print fabric. Black threads enhance all other colors. Once complete, trim and straighten the edges of the crazy-patch piece.*

**2.** To make the bias tube for attaching the chain and closing the button, fold the bias-cut 1" x 6" piece in half, right sides together, and sew the long edge with a ¼" seam allowance. Turn the tube right side out with a large needle and thread or a tube turner.

**3.** Cut the tube into three 2" lengths. Fold one piece in half to make a loop. Pin it in place at the center of the flap, with the raw ends facing outward.

**4.** Place the lining on the quilted crazy-patch piece, right sides together. Referring to figure 1–3, indicate 6¼" down on each side of the flap with a pin. Pin the lining around the flap edge.

**5.** Use a curved object, such as a cup or saucer, to draw the curved corners on the flap. Machine stitch with a ¼" seam allowance around the flap's edge, following the curves at the corners. Backstitch at the beginning and end of the seam at the 6¼" marks.

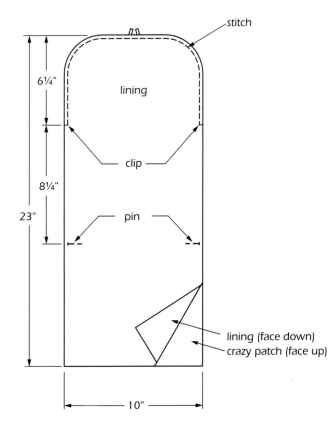

**Fig. 1–3.** Sew around the flap edge.

**6.** Trim the excess fabric at the curves and clip the sides at a right angle where shown in figure 1–3. Turn the flap right side out, revealing the crazy patch and button loop. Stitch approximately ¼" in from the sewn edges of the flap to "set" these edges.

**7.** Measure down 8¼" from the flap fold on each side. Fold the crazy patch and backing to the front and the lining to the back at the 8¼" marks, as shown in figure 1–4. Pin in place and stitch on each side, through all layers, with a ¼" seam allowance (fig. 1–5). The raw edges will extend beyond the flap sides by a full ¼".

**8.** Now the fun part! Reach inside the crazy patch and turn the piece right side out. Voila! Your purse is almost complete.

**9.** From the inside, push the bottom corners outward. Then from the outside, push each corner inward again. Sew across both bottom inside corners, as shown in figure 1–6, to form a base for the purse.

**10.** Fold the remaining raw edges to the inside and pin. For the chain, fold the other two tube pieces into loops and pin them between the raw edges, one on each side of the bag. Stitch across the pinned edge, catching the loops in the stitching as shown in figure 1–6. Sew the button in place and attach the chain to complete the purse.

**RIGHT: Fig. 1–6.** *Sew across the bottom inside corners, fold the raw edges to the inside and pin, add the loops, and sew across the top edge.*

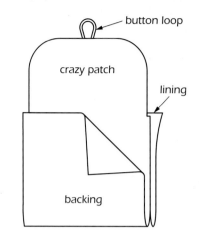

**Fig. 1–4.** *Turn inside-out between crazy patch and lining. Fold crazy patch to the front, lining to the back.*

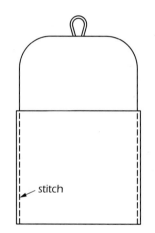

**Fig. 1–5.** *Sew each side through all layers.*

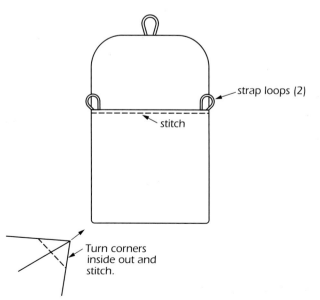

# Box-Style Handbag

## MATERIALS

Planned or unplanned crazy-patch pieces: two 7" squares and a 7" x 8½" rectangle for the flap

Batting and backing cut the same sizes as the crazy-patch pieces

Lining for flap, cut 7" x 8½", and lining for inside handbag, cut 8" x 16"

Novelty button and shoulder chain or decorative strap 33" to 35" long

Bias-cut piece of fabric for loops, 1" x 6"

Side and bottom "sashing" fabric, cut 1½" x 20" (suggest suede, velvet, etc., with a heavy pellon or buckram facing)

Embroidery thread: black or colors to match crazy patch

## Assembly

**1.** For each section of the box, stack the crazy patch, batting, and backing pieces and baste the layers together. Stitching through all three layers, cover the pieced seams with embroidery stitches by hand, machine, or a combination of both.

**2.** To make the bias tube for attaching the chain and closing the button, fold the bias-cut 1" x 6" piece in half, right sides together, and sew the long edge with a ¼" seam allowance. Turn the tube right side out with a large needle and thread or a tube turner.

**3.** Cut the tube into three 2" lengths. Fold one piece in half to make a loop. Pin it in place at the center of the flap, with the raw ends facing outward.

**4.** Place the lining on the flap, right sides together, and sew three sides with a ¼" seam allowance (fig. 1–7). Trim any excess fabric as needed and turn the flap right side out. Stitch approximately ¼" in from the sewn edges of the flap to "set" these edges.

**5.** For the bottom of the purse, find the midpoint of the sashing piece and one side of each of the 7" crazy-patch pieces. Matching midpoints, pin the crazy-patch pieces to the sashing. Sew the pieces together, starting and stopping ¼" from the ends to leave the seam allowances unstitched.

**6.** Clip the seam allowances at a right angle as shown in figure 1–8. Pin the free ends of the sashing to the sides of the crazy-patch pieces and stitch as shown in figure 1–9. A walking foot assists in stitching these layers.

**7.** Gently turn the purse right side out, pushing the bottom corners into place. Pin the flap onto the back of the purse at the top edge. Fold the other two tube pieces into loops and pin them to the sides, raw ends facing upward, between the crazy patch and the lining (fig. 1–10).

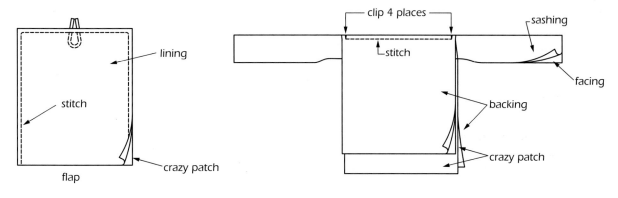

Fig. **1–7.** Sew three sides of the flap.

Fig. **1–8.** Clip the seam allowances.

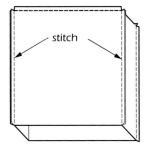

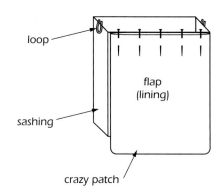

Fig. **1–9.** Sew the sashing to the front and the back of the purse.

Fig. **1–10.** Pin the flap to the back and add the loops.

**8.** Starting on one side of the purse, wrap the lining around the outside, right sides together, and pin along the top (fig. 1–11). Join the ends of the lining with a ¼" seam allowance. Then sew all around the top (fig. 1–12).

**9.** Pull the lining upward so it is right side out and sew across the raw edge of the lining (fig. 1–13). Push the lining down into the purse. Hand or machine sew the lining in place along the purse top ¼" in from the edge. Finish by sewing on the button and adding a chain or strap.

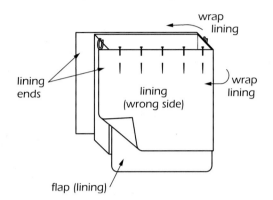

**Fig. 1–11.** Wrap the lining around the purse and sew the lining ends together to make a tube.

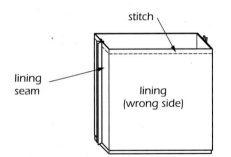

**Fig. 1–12.** Sew around the top of the purse.

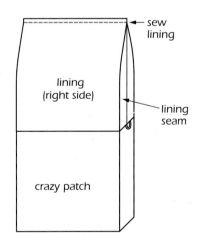

**Fig. 1–13.** Pull the lining up and sew across the edge.

TEACHING SAMPLER, 92½" x 123", by the author.

The quilters' alphabet from A to Z, stitched on my embroidery module, was used to embellish the accent border between the sampler blocks on this colorful quilt. I used this alphabet on my *Lap Quilting* television program, series 1100, giving an explanation of quilters' lingo on each of the 13 shows (see Quilters' Alphabet, page 155). A range of three sizes of blocks allows color exploration and setting options. Note that this quilt makes a good width for a queen- or king-sized bed, and it is extra long. If you want a shorter quilt, you can eliminate one horizontal row.

**Quilt size, 92½" x 123"**
**18 different blocks, sizes 6", 12", and 18"**

## MATERIALS

| FABRIC | YARDS | CUTTING |
|---|---|---|
| Light (lt) background | 4 total | See chart, pgs. 23–27 |
| Dark (dk) | 3½ total | See chart, pgs. 23–27 |
| Contrast (con) | 1 total | See chart, pgs. 23–27 |
| Other (oth) | 1 total | See chart, pgs. 23–27 |
| Light (lt) | 1½ | Diamond blocks & C rectangles |
| Striped sashing & border | 1 | 1" wide strips |
| Backing | 3¾, if 108" wide 11¼, if pieced | |
| Binding | 1 | 2½" wide strips |
| Batting | | 100" x 130" |

## Rotary-Cut Blocks

The following chart provides the measurements (seam allowances included) for rotary cutting and piecing 18 traditional blocks in three different sizes: 6", 12", and 18". Now you have a choice to adapt these various-sized blocks to your wallhangings or larger quilts.

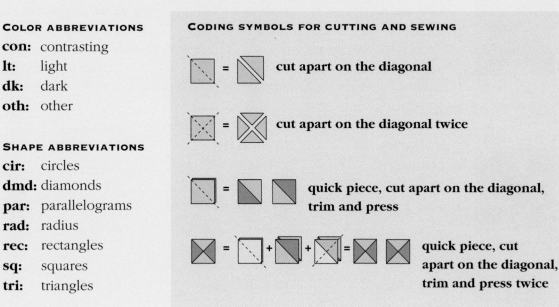

## Symbol and Abbreviation Key
for Cutting Instructions chart (23–27)

**COLOR ABBREVIATIONS**

**con:** contrasting
**lt:** light
**dk:** dark
**oth:** other

**SHAPE ABBREVIATIONS**

**cir:** circles
**dmd:** diamonds
**par:** parallelograms
**rad:** radius
**rec:** rectangles
**sq:** squares
**tri:** triangles

**CODING SYMBOLS FOR CUTTING AND SEWING**

= cut apart on the diagonal

= cut apart on the diagonal twice

= quick piece, cut apart on the diagonal, trim and press

= quick piece, cut apart on the diagonal, trim and press twice

# CUTTING INSTRUCTIONS

**6" Double Four-Patch**

2 oth sq 3½"
4 lt sq 2"
4 dk sq 2"

**12" Double Four-Patch**

2 oth sq 6½"
4 lt sq 3½"
4 dk sq 3½"

**18" Double Four-Patch**

2 oth sq 9½"
4 lt sq 5"
4 dk sq 5"

**6" Nine-Patch**

5 lt sq 2½"
4 dk sq 2½"

**12" Nine-Patch**

5 lt sq 4½"
4 dk sq 4½"

**18" Nine-Patch**

5 lt sq 6½"
4 dk sq 6½"

**6" Star Flower**

4 dk sq 2"
2 lt & 2 dk sq 2⅜"
2 dk & 2 oth sq 2⅜"
2 lt & 2 oth sq 2⅜"

**12" Star Flower**

4 dk sq 3½"
2 lt & 2 dk sq 3⅞"
2 dk & 2 oth sq 3⅞"
2 lt & 2 oth sq 3⅞"

**18" Star Flower**

4 dk sq 5"
2 lt & 2 dk sq 5⅜"
2 dk & 2 oth sq 5⅜"
2 lt & 2 oth sq 5⅜"

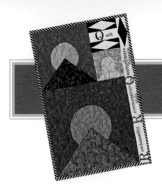

### 6" King's X
4 oth sq 2⅜"
2 lt sq 3⅞"
(Cut strip 1⅝" wide from tri.)
2 dk sq 3⅞"
(Cut strip 1⅝" wide from tri.)

### 12" King's X
4 oth sq 3⅞"
2 lt sq 6⅞"
(Cut strip 2⅝" wide from tri.)
2 dk sq 6⅞"
(Cut strip 2⅝" wide from tri.)

### 18" King's X
4 oth sq 5⅜"
2 lt sq 9⅞"
(Cut strip 3⅝" wide from tri.)
2 dk sq 9⅞"
(Cut strip 3⅝" wide from tri.)

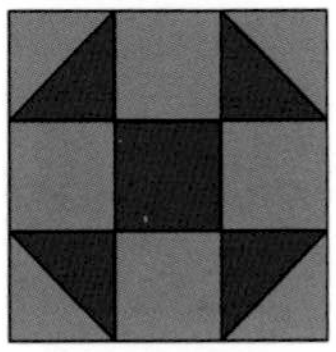

### 6" Shoo Fly
1 dk sq 2½"
4 lt sq 2½"
2 lt & 2 dk sq 2⅞"

### 12" Shoo Fly
1 dk sq 4½"
4 lt sq 4½"
2 lt & 2 dk sq 4⅞"

### 18" Shoo Fly
1 dk sq 6½"
4 lt sq 6½"
2 lt & 2 dk sq 6⅞"

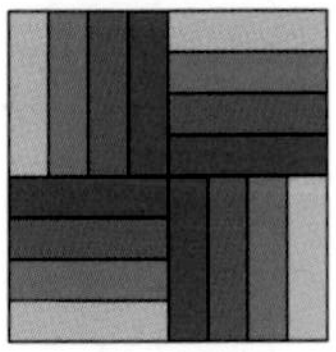

### 6" Rail Fence
4 lt rec 1¼" x 3½"
4 dk rec 1¼" x 3½"
4 oth rec 1¼" x 3½"
4 con rec 1¼" x 3½"

### 12" Rail Fence
4 lt rec 2" x 6½"
4 dk rec 2" x 6½"
4 oth rec 2" x 6½"
4 con rec 2" x 6½"

### 18" Rail Fence
4 lt rec 2¾" x 9½"
4 dk rec 2¾" x 9½"
4 oth rec 2¾" x 9½"
4 con rec 2¾" x 9½"

### 6" Jacob's Ladder
2 lt & 2 dk sq 2⅞"
10 lt sq 1½"
10 dk sq 1½"

### 12" Jacob's Ladder
2 lt & 2 dk sq 4⅞"
10 lt sq 2½"
10 dk sq 2½"

### 18" Jacob's Ladder
2 lt & 2 dk sq 6⅞"
10 lt sq 3½"
10 dk sq 3½"

### 6" Monkey Wrench
2 dk sq 1⅝"
2 lt sq 1⅝"
1 lt sq 2⅜"
1 dk sq 2⅜"
1 lt sq 3"
1 dk sq 3"
1 lt sq 3⅞"
1 dk sq 3⅞"

### 12" Monkey Wrench
2 dk sq 2⅝"
2 lt sq 2⅝"
1 lt sq 3⅞"
1 dk sq 3⅞"
1 lt sq 5⅛"
1 dk sq 5⅛"
1 lt sq 6⅞"
1 dk sq 6⅞"

### 18" Monkey Wrench
2 dk sq 3¾"
2 lt sq 3¾"
1 lt sq 5⅜"
1 dk sq 5⅜"
1 lt sq 7¼"
1 dk sq 7¼"
1 lt sq 9⅞"
1 dk sq 9⅞"

### 6" Ohio Star
4 dk sq 2½"
1 lt sq 2½"
2 lt & 2 dk sq 3¼"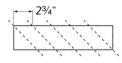

### 12" Ohio Star
4 dk sq 4½"
1 lt sq 4½"
2 lt & 2 dk sq 5¼"

### 18" Ohio Star
4 dk sq 6½"
1 lt sq 6½"
2 lt & 2 dk sq 7¼"

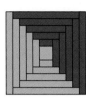

### 6" Log Cabin
1 lt sq 1½"
1 lt rec 1" x 1½"
1 lt & 1 dk rec 1" x 2"
1 lt & 1 dk rec 1" x 2½"
1 lt & 1 dk rec 1" x 3"
1 lt & 1 dk rec 1" x 3½"
1 lt & 1 dk rec 1" x 4"
1 lt & 1 dk rec 1" x 4½"
1 lt & 1 dk rec 1" x 5"
1 lt & 1 dk rec 1" x 5½"
1 lt & 1 dk rec 1" x 6"
1 dk rec 1" x 6½"

### 12" Log Cabin
1 lt sq 2½"
1 lt rec 1½" x 2½"
1 lt & 1 dk rec 1½" x 3½"
1 lt & 1 dk rec 1½" x 4½"
1 lt & 1 dk rec 1½" x 5½"
1 lt & 1 dk rec 1½" x 6½"
1 lt & 1 dk rec 1½" x 7½"
1 lt & 1 dk rec 1½" x 8½"
1 lt & 1 dk rec 1½" x 9½"
1 lt & 1 dk rec 1½" x 10½"
1 lt & 1 dk rec 1½" x 11½"
1 dk rec 1½" x 12½"

### 18" Log Cabin
1 lt sq 3½"
1 lt rec 1¾" x 3½"
1 lt & 1 dk rec 1¾" x 4¾"
1 lt & 1 dk rec 1¾" x 6"
1 lt & 1 dk rec 1¾" x 7¼"
1 lt & 1 dk rec 1¾" x 8½"
1 lt & 1 dk rec 1¾" x 9¾"
1 lt & 1 dk rec 1¾" x 11"
1 lt & 1 dk rec 1¾" x 12¼"
1 lt & 1 dk rec 1¾" x 13½"
1 lt & 1 dk rec 1¾" x 14¾"
1 lt & 1 dk rec 1¾" x 16"
1 lt & 1 dk rec 1¾" x 17¼"
1 dk rec 1¾" x 18½"

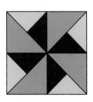

### 6" Pin Wheel
1 lt & 1 dk sq 4¼"
2 oth sq 3⅞"

### 12" Pin Wheel
1 lt & 1 dk sq 7¼"
2 oth sq 6⅞"

### 18" Pin Wheel
1 lt & 1 dk sq 10¼"
2 oth sq 9⅞"

### 6" Formal Garden
1 lt sq 2½"
1 dk sq 5¼"
1 lt strip 2½" x 14"
(Cut into 4 par.)

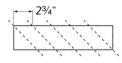

### 12" Formal Garden
1 lt sq 4½"
1 dk sq 9¼"
1 lt strip 4½" x 24"
(Cut into 4 par.)

### 18" Formal Garden
1 lt sq 6½"
1 dk sq 13¼"
1 lt strip 6½" x 34"
(Cut into 4 par.)

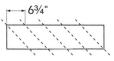

‹— 2¾"

‹— 4¾"

‹— 6¾"

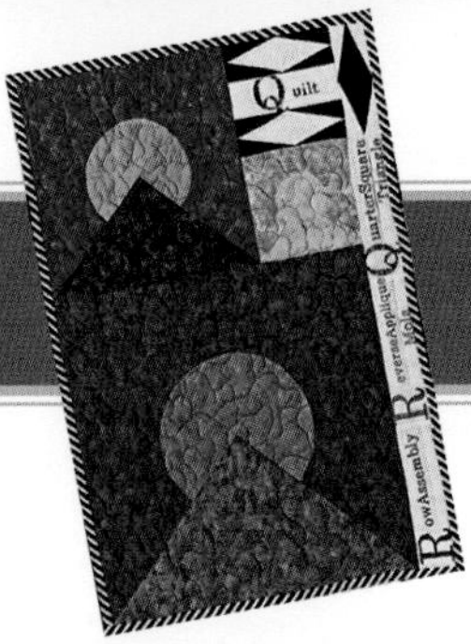

# Teaching Sampler

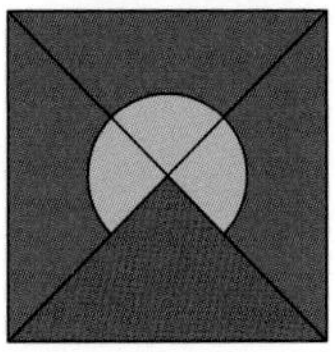

| 6" Moon Over Mount. | 12" Moon Over Mount. | 18" Moon Over Mount. |
|---|---|---|
| 3 lt tri with 7¼" base (sky) | 3 lt tri with 13¼" base (sky) | 3 lt tri with 19¼" base (sky) |
| (From the right angle, remove 1½" rad cir.) | (From the right angle, remove 3" rad cir.) | (From the right angle, remove 5" rad cir.) |
| 1 dk tri with 7¼" base (mtn) | 1 dk tri with 13¼" base (mtn) | 1 dk tri with 19¼" base (mtn) |
| 3 lt quarter cir 2" rad (moon) | 3 lt quarter cir 3½" rad (moon) | 3 lt quarter cir 5½" rad (moon) |

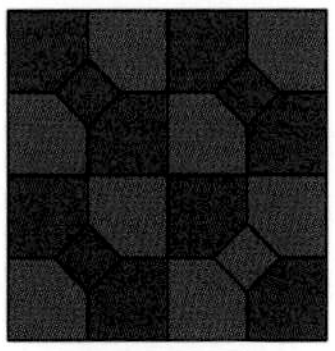

| 6" Bow Tie | 12" Bow Tie | 18" Bow Tie |
|---|---|---|
| 8 lt & 8 dk sq 2" | 8 lt & 8 dk sq 3½" | 8 lt & 8 dk sq 5" |
| Measure short sides. | Measure short sides. | Measure short sides. |
| (Clip ⅞" triangle from 1 corner of each sq.) | (Clip 1⅝" triangle from 1 corner of each sq.) | (Clip 2¼" triangle from 1 corner of each sq.) |
| 2 lt & 2 dk sq 1½" | 2 lt & 2 dk sq 2½" | 2 lt & 2 dk sq 3½" |

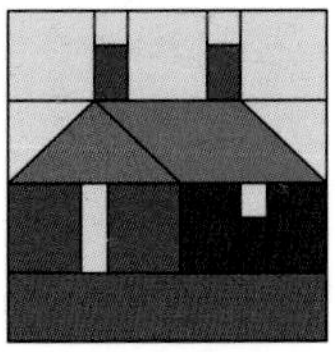

| 6" House on the Hill | 12" House on the Hill | 18" House on the Hill |
|---|---|---|
| 3 lt sq 2" | 3 lt sq 3½" | 3 lt sq 5" |
| 3 lt sq 1¼" | 3 lt sq 2" | 3 lt sq 2¾" |
| 2 con sq 1¼" | 2 con sq 2" | 2 con sq 2¾" |
| 1 lt sq 2⅜" | 1 lt sq 3⅞" | 1 lt sq 5⅜" |
| 2 dk rec 1⅝" x 2¼" | 2 dk rec 2¾" x 4" | 2 dk rec 3⅞" x 5¾" |
| 2 oth rec 1⅝" x 2¼" | 2 oth rec 2¾" x 4" | 2 oth rec 3⅞" x 5¾" |
| 1 oth rec 1¼" x 1½" | 1 oth rec 2" x 2½" | 1 oth rec 2¾" x 3½" |
| 1 oth rec 1¼" x 2¼" | 1 oth rec 2" x 4" | 1 oth rec 2¾" x 5¾" |
| 1 con rec 1¾" x 6½" | 1 con rec 3" x 12½" | 1 con rec 4¼" x 18½" |
| 1 con tri with 4¼" base | 1 con tri with 7¼" base | 1 con tri with 10¼" base |
| 1 dk par 3¾" base x 2" high | 1 dk par 6¾" base x 3½" high | 1 dk par 9¾" base x 5" high |

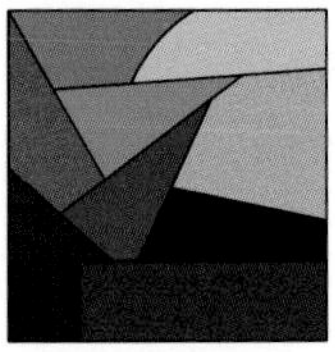

| 6" Crazy Patch | 12" Crazy Patch | 18" Crazy Patch |
|---|---|---|
| **PLANNED** (Instructions, page 13) | | |
| 6" iron-on grid paper sq (Cut into templates.) | 12" iron-on grid paper sq (Cut into templates.) | 18" iron-on grid paper sq (Cut into templates.) |
| **UNPLANNED** (Instructions, page 14) | | |
| 7" foundation sq (Stitch and flip, trim block to 6½".) | 13" foundation sq (Stitch and flip, trim block to 12½".) | 19" foundation sq (Stitch and flip, trim block to 18½".) |

**6" Dresden Plate**
(Wedge patterns, page 31)
16 wedges, assorted fabrics
1 lt sq 6½"
1 con cir 1¼" rad

**12" Dresden Plate**

16 wedges, assorted fabrics
1 lt sq 12½"
1 con cir 2¼" rad

**18" Dresden Plate**

16 wedges, assorted fabrics
1 lt sq 18½"
1 con cir 3¼" rad

**6" Grandmother's Fan**
(Wedge patterns, page 31)
8 wedges, assorted fabrics
1 lt sq 6½"
1 con quarter cir 2⅛"

**12" Grandmother's Fan**

8 wedges, assorted fabrics
1 lt sq 12½"
1 con quarter cir 4¼"

**18" Grandmother's Fan**

8 wedges, assorted fabrics
1 lt sq 18½"sq
1 con quarter cir 6¼"

## POINTED FAN WEDGES

**1.** To create pointed ends for the Dresden Plate and Grandmother's Fan wedges, add the following lengths to the wide end of each wedge template: 6" block, add ½"; 12" block, 1"; and 18" block, 1½" (fig. 1–14).

**2.** Cut the template on the solid line.

**3.** Use the template to cut the fabric wedges needed for your quilt.

**4.** Fold each fabric wedge in half lengthwise, right sides together.

**5.** Use a ¼" seam allowance to sew across the top of the wedge and trim the right angle as shown (fig. 1–15).

**6.** Unfold the wedge and gently push out the point. After the wedges are sewn together, attach the circle (Dresden Plate) or quarter circle (Grandmother's Fan) to the foundation with a running stitch or decorative stitch.

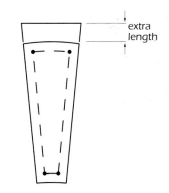

extra
length

**Fig. 1–14.** For pointed ends, add extra length to the wedge patterns.

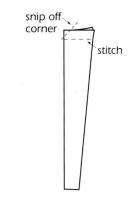

snip off
corner

stitch

**Fig. 1–15.** Sew and trim the wide end of the wedge.

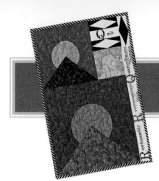

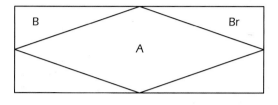

**Fig. 1–16.** Diamond block and C rectangle.

## Quilt Assembly

To make the quilt shown in the photograph, (page 21) refer to the chart on pages 23–27.

**1.** Sew one of each block, in all three sizes, for a total of 54 blocks. Make 56 diamond blocks and C rectangles as needed (fig. 1–16) from the patterns on page 30.

**2.** Embellish the blocks as desired. An embroidery machine alphabet was used to enhance this quilt.

**3.** Referring to the quilt assembly diagram on page 29, assemble the blocks into sections, including diamond blocks and light C rectangles (fig. 1–17).

**4.** Piece lengths of 1" wide striped sashing together, end to end, as needed. Sew block sections together, inserting striped sashing between the sections.

*Notice that there is no striped sashing between the House on the Hill and the Dresden Plate sections in the lower-right corner of the quilt.*

**5.** Add a striped border to the quilt. You can use butted or mitered corners for your border.

**6.** Layer, baste, and quilt the layers, then bind the raw edges and add a label to complete your quilt.

**Fig. 1–17.** Quilt assembly.

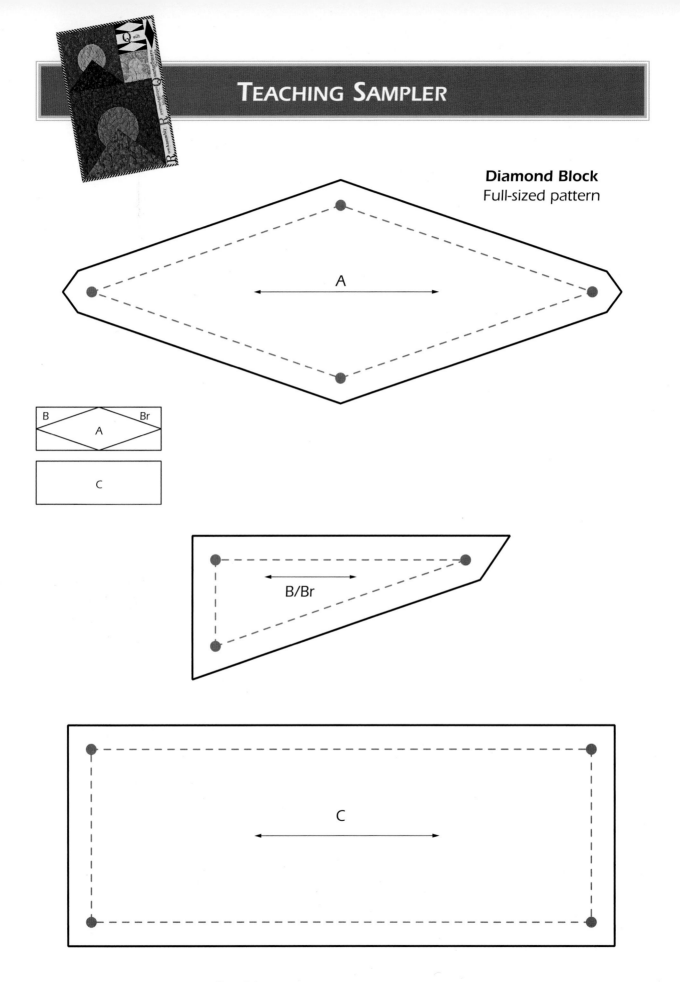

**Diamond Block**
Full-sized pattern

A

B    Br
A

C

B/Br

C

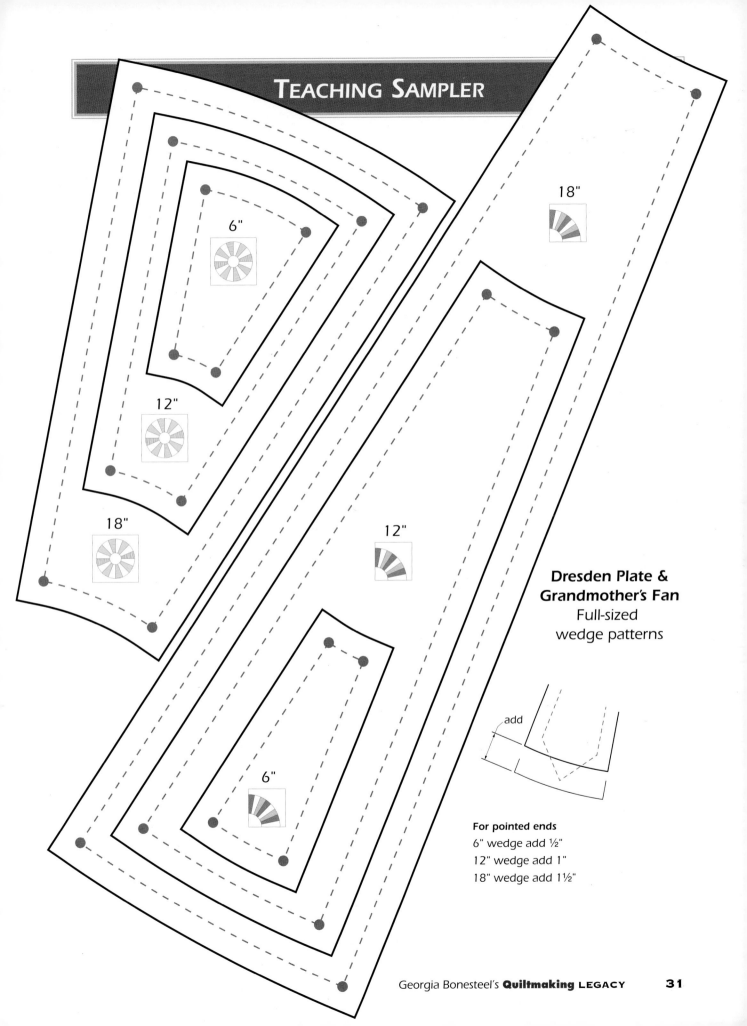

6"

12"

18"

18"

12"

6"

**Dresden Plate &
Grandmother's Fan**
Full-sized
wedge patterns

add

**For pointed ends**
6" wedge add ½"
12" wedge add 1"
18" wedge add 1½"

COUNTRY TO COUNTRY SAMPLER, 54" x 54", by the author.

# Country to Country Sampler

In the COUNTRY TO COUNTRY SAMPLER, 6" blocks are sewn around a fabric panel of your choosing. Each block in the quilt in the photo depicts a show theme from the 13-week television 1100 series, but you can experiment with this setting for any of your favorite 6" blocks. Add a signature block at the center bottom of the quilt or make another 6" block of your choice for that spot.

**Quilt size: 54" x 54"**

## MATERIALS

Theme (center panel): 1 yard

Assorted coordinated scraps for 13 blocks, 6" x 6"

Sashing strips: ½ yard

Dark fabric (squares and triangles): ⅔ yard

Light fabric (squares and triangles): 1 yard

## Cutting

**Center panel:** 24½" x 24½"

**Sashing:** 14 strips 2½" x 6½"
14 strips 2½" x 8½"

**Squares:** 1 square, 8½", from theme fabric
1 square, 6½", for signature block

4 squares, 4½", from theme fabric
20 squares, 4½", from light fabric

**Triangles:**

5 pairs of contrasting squares, 4⅞", for 10 half-square triangle units

7 pairs of contrasting squares, 5¼", for 14 quarter-square triangle units

**White inner border:**

2 side strips 1½" x 48½"
top and bottom strips 1½" x 50½"

**Outer border squares:**

52 dark squares 2½"
52 light squares 2½"

## Block Assembly

Make thirteen 6" blocks from the patterns provided on pages 36–48. Make a fourteenth block of your choice if you want to replace the signature block.

Rotary-cutting measurements are given for those patches that can be rotary cut. You will need to make templates for the patches that cannot be rotary cut and for the appliquéd blocks.

## Country to Country Sampler

### Quilt Assembly

**1.** Use quick-piecing to make 10 half-square triangle units and 14 quarter-square triangle units.

**2.** Referring to the quilt assembly diagram (fig. 1–18), arrange the 6½" blocks around the theme panel and place the sashing strips on two adjacent sides of each block. Add the squares and triangle units to the arrangement.

**3.** When you are satisfied with the arrangement, sew the sashing strips to the blocks.

**4.** Sew the pieces together in rows, then sew the rows together to complete the body of the quilt. Add the white inner border strips.

**5.** Alternating dark and light, sew the outer border squares together to make four border strips. Sew the strips to the quilt. Hand quilting completes this wallhanging.

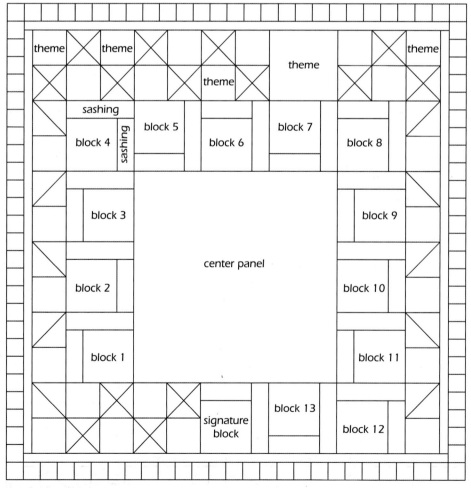

**Fig. 1–18.** Quilt assembly.

Rotary-cutting measurements are given for those patches that lend themselves to this technique. See page 23 for rotary-cutting symbols.

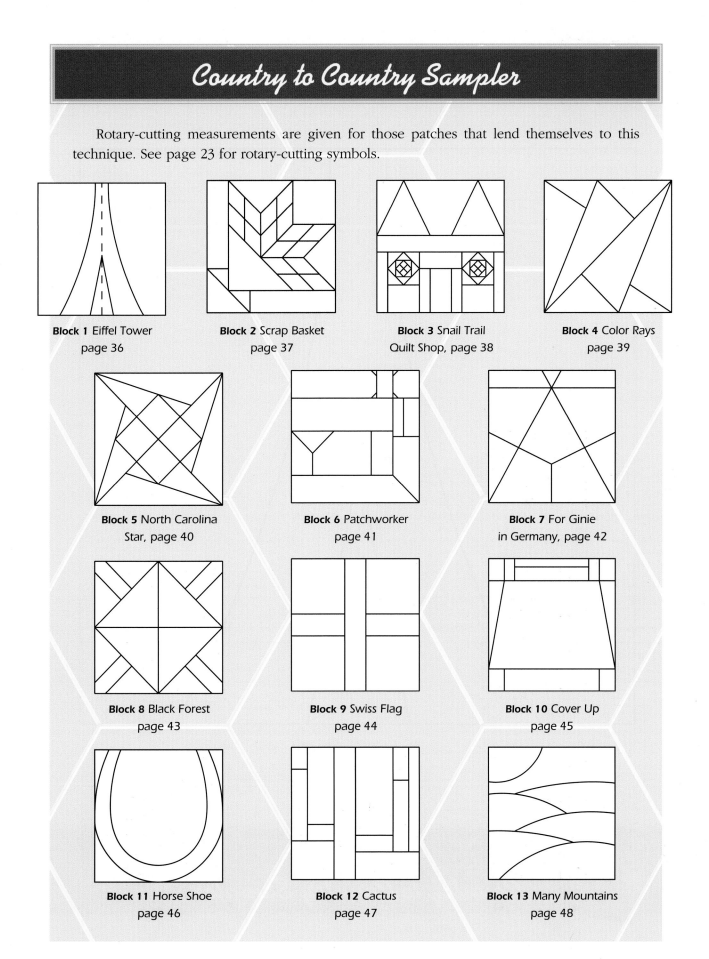

**Block 1** Eiffel Tower
page 36

**Block 2** Scrap Basket
page 37

**Block 3** Snail Trail
Quilt Shop, page 38

**Block 4** Color Rays
page 39

**Block 5** North Carolina
Star, page 40

**Block 6** Patchworker
page 41

**Block 7** For Ginie
in Germany, page 42

**Block 8** Black Forest
page 43

**Block 9** Swiss Flag
page 44

**Block 10** Cover Up
page 45

**Block 11** Horse Shoe
page 46

**Block 12** Cactus
page 47

**Block 13** Many Mountains
page 48

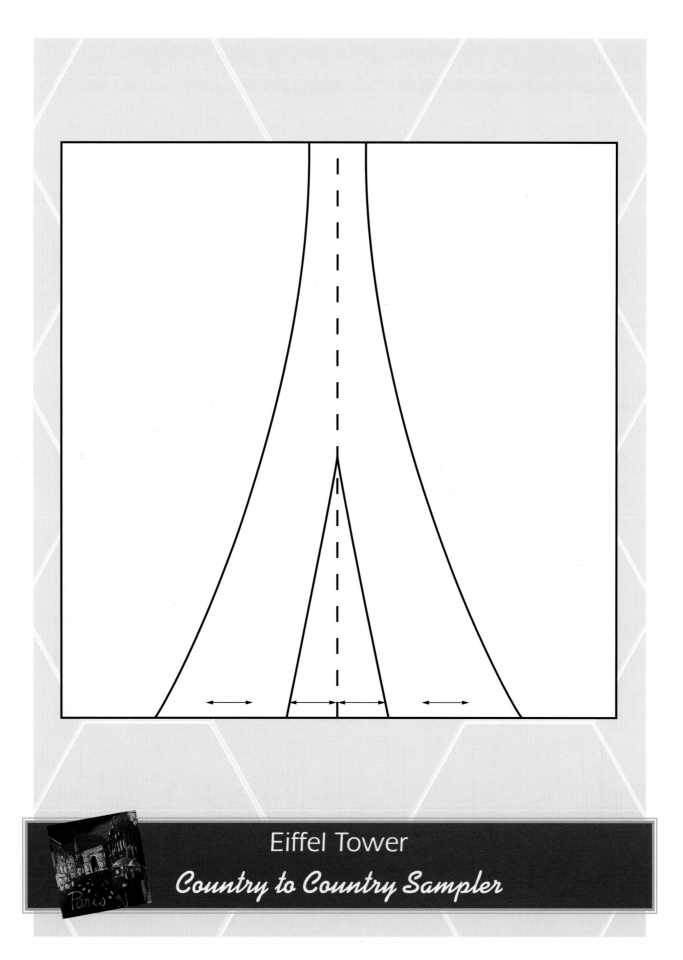

Eiffel Tower

*Country to Country Sampler*

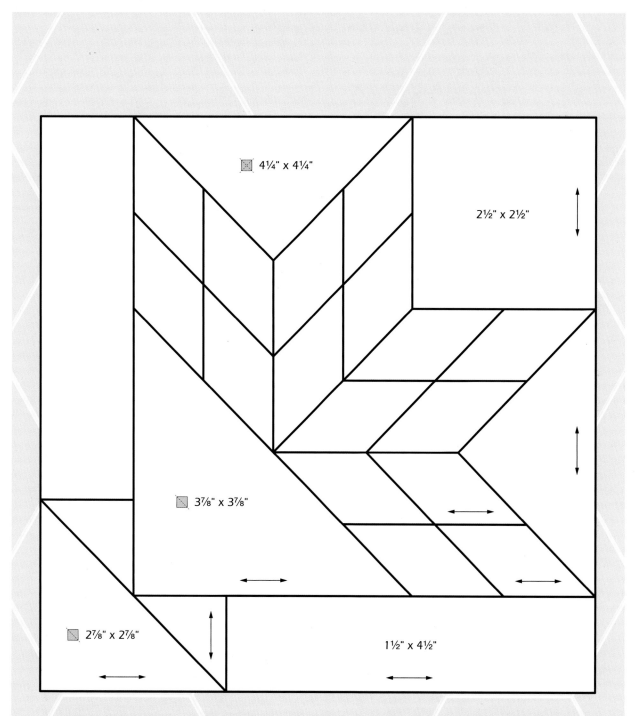

4¼" x 4¼"

2½" x 2½"

3⅞" x 3⅞"

2⅞" x 2⅞"

1½" x 4½"

To make the diamonds, cut dark and light contrasting strips 1¼" x 18". Sew a dark and a light strip together to make a strip-set. Cut the strip-set every 1¼" at a 45-degree angle to make pairs of diamonds.

# Scrap Basket
## *Country to Country Sampler*

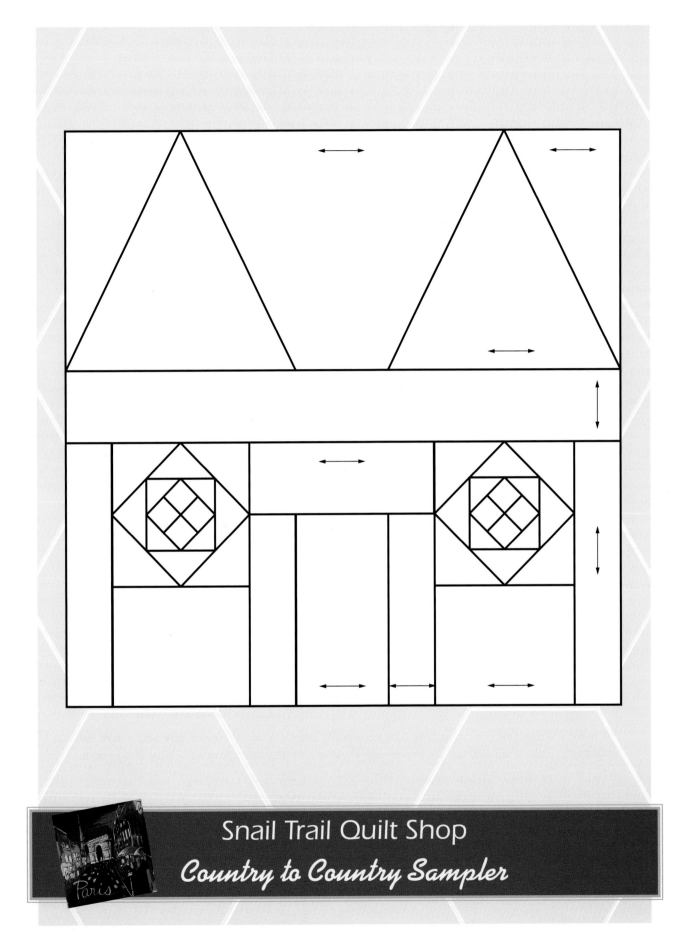

Snail Trail Quilt Shop

*Country to Country Sampler*

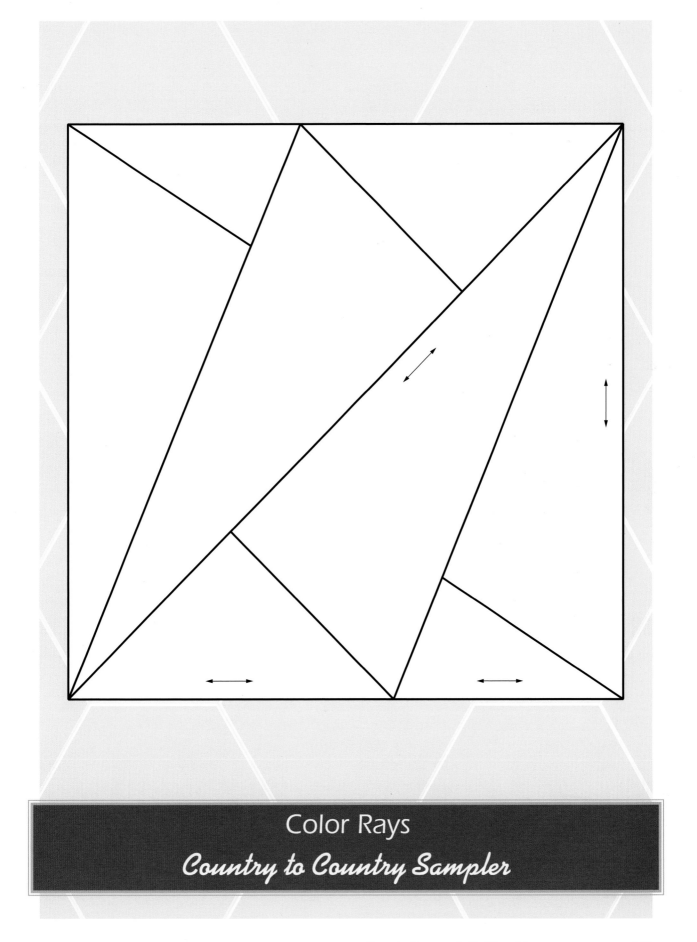

Color Rays

*Country to Country Sampler*

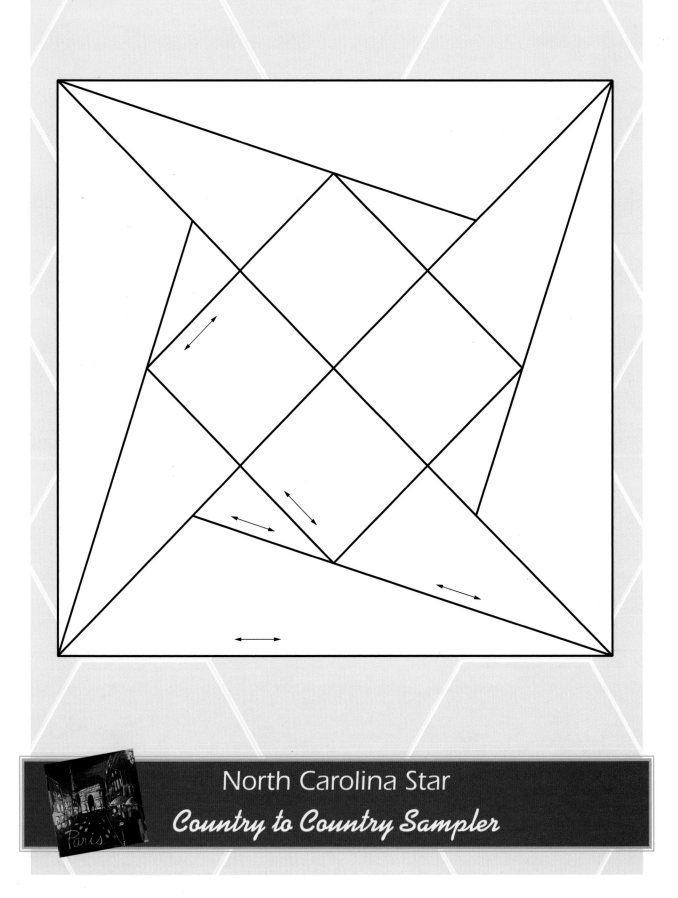

North Carolina Star

*Country to Country Sampler*

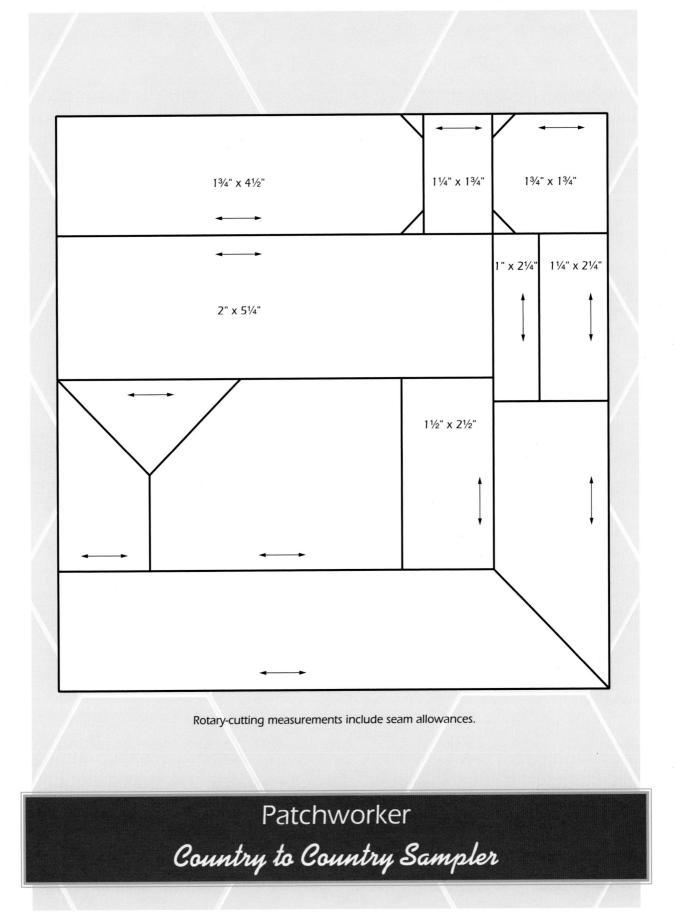

1¾" x 4½"

1¼" x 1¾"

1¾" x 1¾"

2" x 5¼"

1" x 2¼"

1¼" x 2¼"

1½" x 2½"

Rotary-cutting measurements include seam allowances.

# Patchworker
## Country to Country Sampler

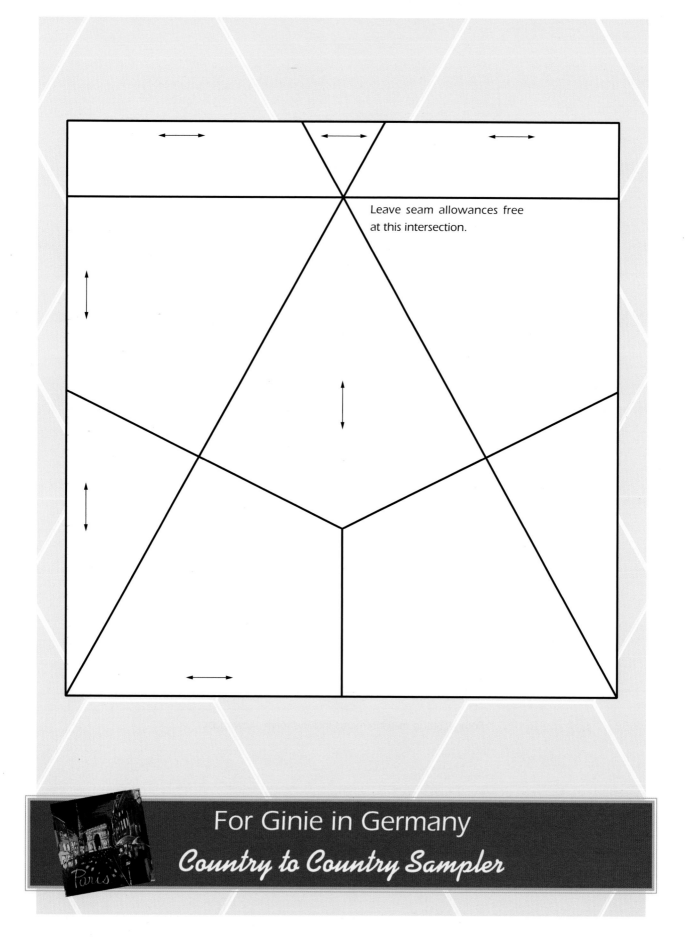

Leave seam allowances free
at this intersection.

For Ginie in Germany

*Country to Country Sampler*

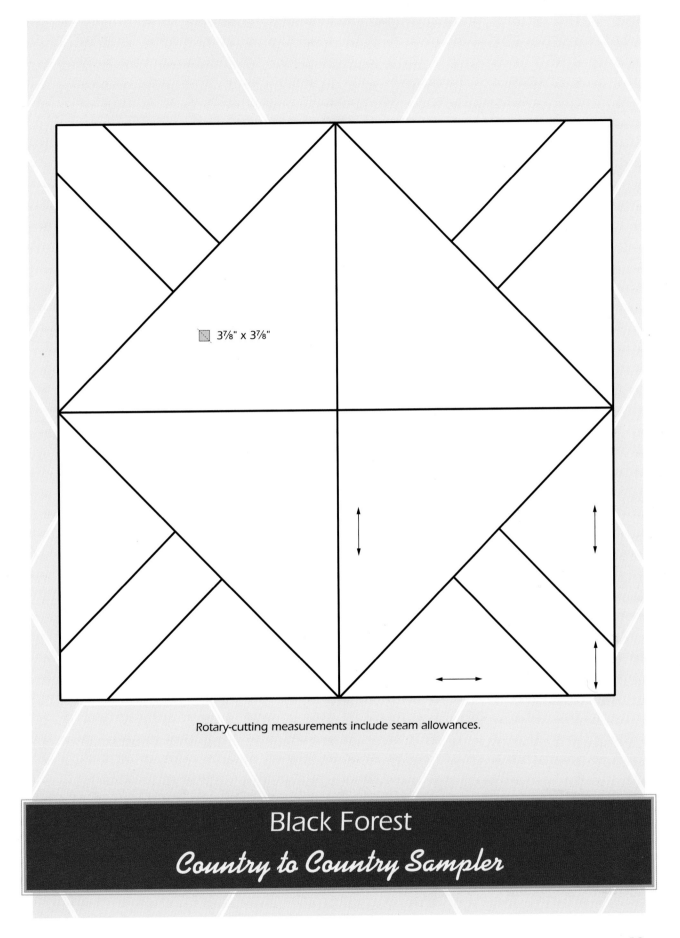

3⅞" x 3⅞"

Rotary-cutting measurements include seam allowances.

## Black Forest
*Country to Country Sampler*

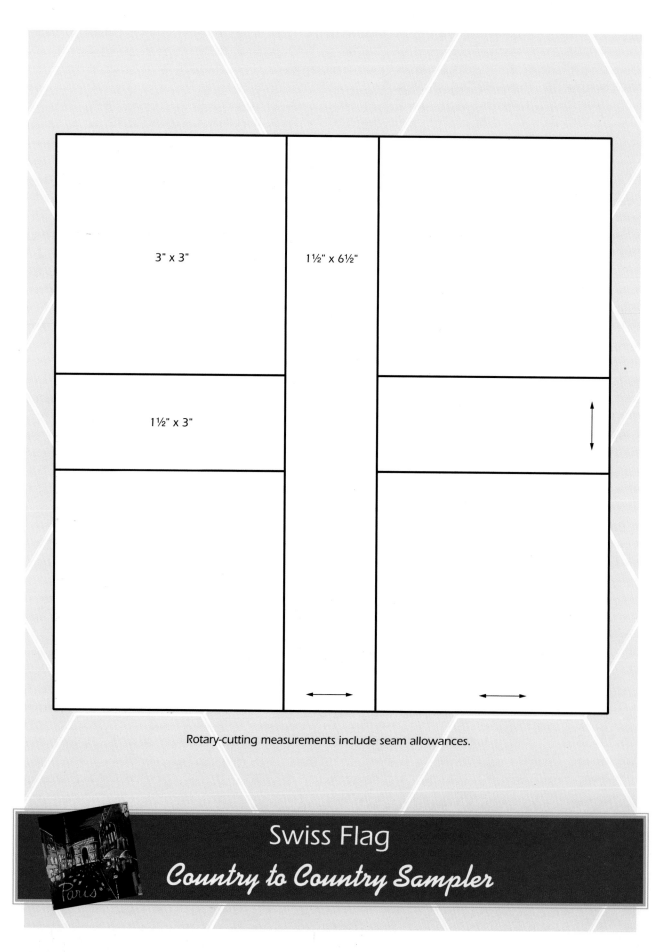

3" x 3"

1½" x 6½"

1½" x 3"

Rotary-cutting measurements include seam allowances.

## Swiss Flag
*Country to Country Sampler*

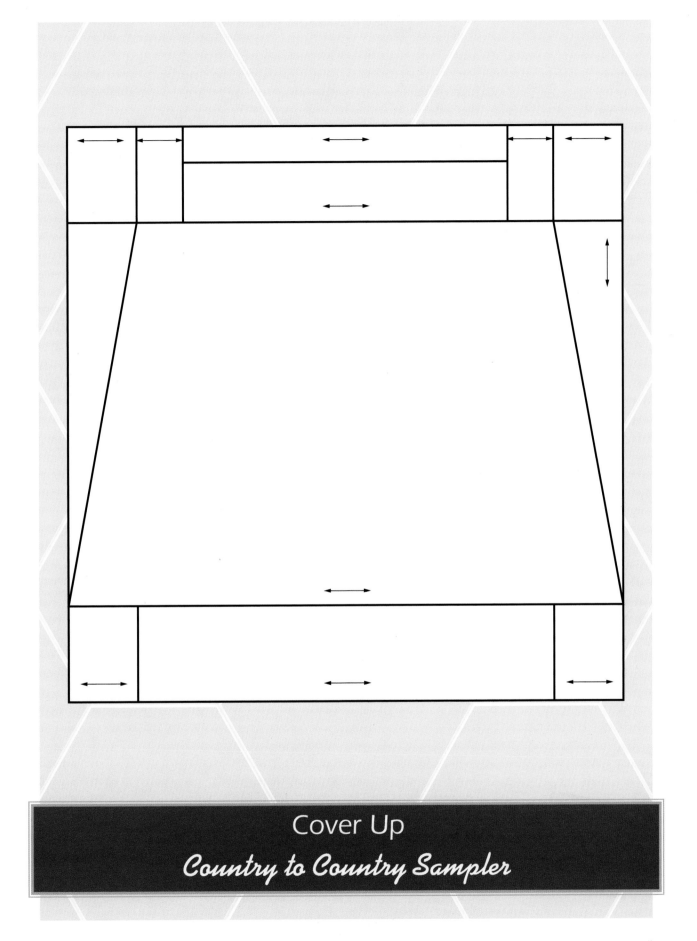

## Cover Up

*Country to Country Sampler*

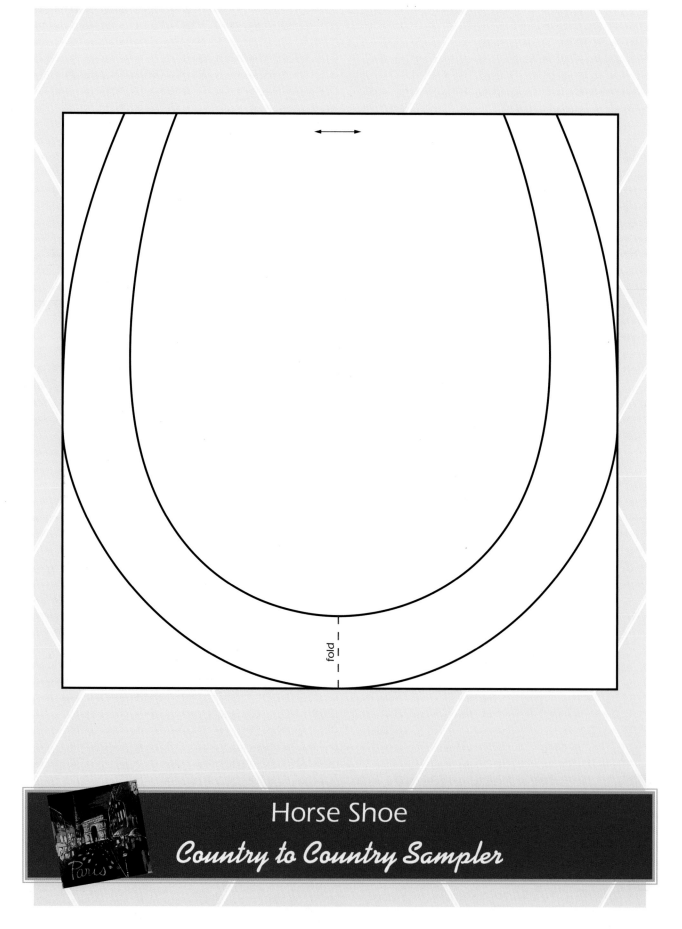

fold

Horse Shoe

*Country to Country Sampler*

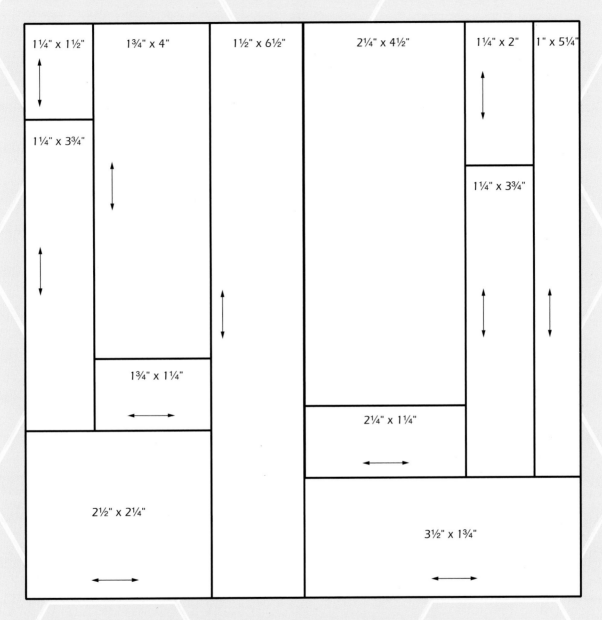

1¼" x 1½"

1¾" x 4"

1½" x 6½"

2¼" x 4½"

1¼" x 2"

1" x 5¼"

1¼" x 3¾"

1¼" x 3¾"

1¾" x 1¼"

2¼" x 1¼"

2½" x 2¼"

3½" x 1¾"

Rotary-cutting measurements include seam allowances.

# Cactus
## *Country to Country Sampler*

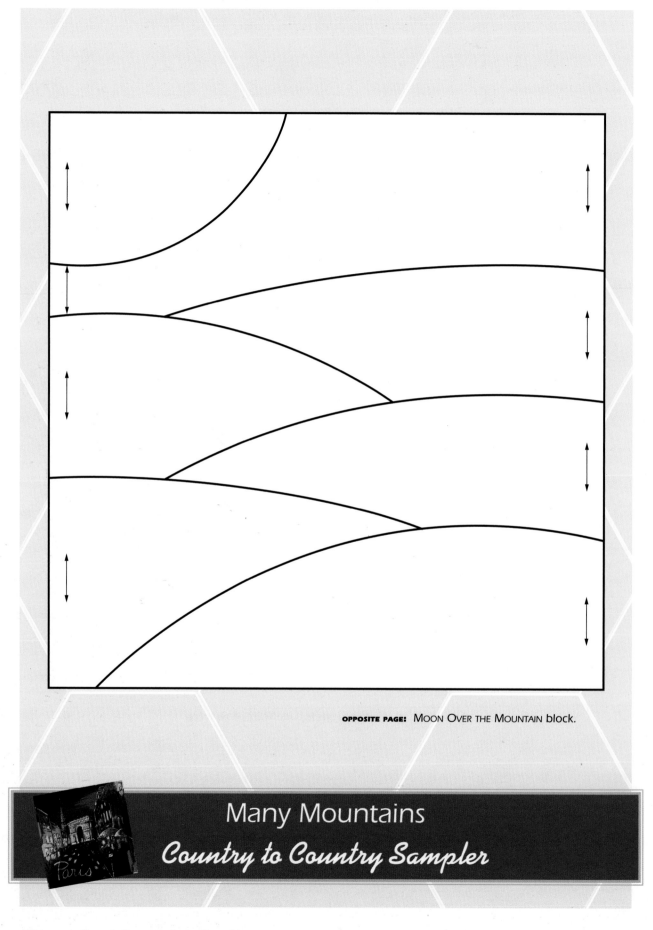

**OPPOSITE PAGE:** MOON OVER THE MOUNTAIN block.

## Many Mountains
### Country to Country Sampler

# Chapter 2

# So Glad I'm Back,

**ABOVE:** Moon Over the Mountain framed.
**OPPOSITE PAGE:** MOON OVER THE MOUNTAIN wallhanging.

How many ways can you make mountains? I have tried them all, from the simple Moon Over the Mountains to mountains made of diamond shapes. They gather together nature's colors in various peaks and valleys and bring me home.

My very first circuit-rider teaching trip was not on a horse. It was on a plane to Tennessee. I remember the fine reception, the excitement of sharing, and the exchanging of ideas. What I particularly recall is getting off the plane back home in Asheville, North Carolina. You see, this was the first time I had taken my quilts on a journey. My logic was to keep them as close to me as I could on the plane, so rather than checking them in with the luggage, I used a garment bag, which the flight attendant hung right inside the door. Upon returning, I disembarked, walked into the terminal, and suddenly noticed my naked arms. I ran back across the tarmac, banged on a closed door, and luckily secured the quilts. People often ask me, "How do you travel with your quilts?" Now, I check them. It's all about trust.

On another flight going west to Oregon, a flight attendant eyed my needle and thread as I worked on a quilted vest. She immediately sat down right next to me with her show-and-tell photo album of quilts. She said that the first thing she did on her layovers was to check the quilt shops in the yellow pages – a dividend for the quilter flight attendant.

Here's a quilter's tip for long flights. Wear a WIP (works in progress) vest on board, one that's already prepared for stitching. Upon leav-

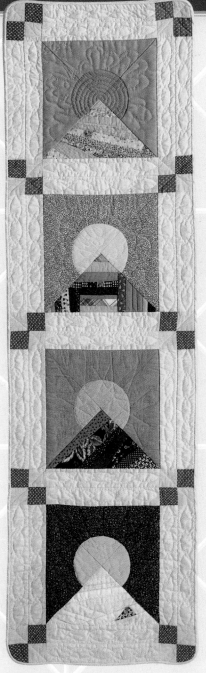

ing the plane, you will have a completed vest. Yet another flight on a small jet from Denver to Riverton, Wyoming, gave me some very anxious moments. Strange squeaking noises right behind my seat made me fear, through the whole flight, that there was something wrong with the plane. When we landed, mixed in with the passengers' luggage were cartons of baby chicks and mice. I gladly helped the local postman wrestle these boxes into his truck before I met with the Wyoming Star Quilters Guild. During that same trip, I was driven far out into the country to a famous drugstore for a peanut butter malt.

I recall a particular memory from Lake of the Ozarks, where I worked for Wal-Mart®. I had flown on a plane so small that my Singer® Featherweight sewing machine was balanced on my shoulders, which would certainly not be permitted today. I taught in a huge underground parking lot and even got to meet Wal-Mart CEO Sam Walton when I was seated at the head table for a banquet.

One afternoon, there was a request for someone to play tennis with Mrs. Walton after class. She was several years older than me, and I certainly did not want to embarrass her on the courts. Well, as it happened, I spent two hours apologizing to her because I missed many of her shots and could hardly return her serves. Mrs. Walton was a very good tennis player, and I have the distinction of being beaten by her!

Coming home for me means the nesting security of family and friends and the creative space in my studio. Surrounding all of this are the beautiful Blue Ridge Mountains, which often recur my designs. In these mountains, I am often reminded of the expression, "A straight line is a line of duty, while a curved line is a line of beauty."

## Strip-Picture Piecing

### My Class Sample
### and
### The Veil in the Tetons

**ABOVE:** My Class Sample, 38" x 28", by the author.
**BELOW:** The Veil in the Tetons, 50" x 40", by the author.

**W**hen teaching this technique, I often refer to it as interrupted rectangles. Just think of the opportunities here – flowers, letters, animals, and naturally, mountains. You start with a grid, establish your lines, draw a simple picture, stitch, and press. The following system works with either of the two strip-picture pieces, THE VEIL IN THE TETONS or MY CLASS SAMPLE.

**MY CLASS SAMPLE, 38" x 28"**

**THE VEIL IN THE TETONS, 50" x 40"**

## MATERIALS FOR EACH PROJECT

Iron-on grid sheet: 20" x 30"

Sky: 1 yard

Star and moon accents: ¼ yard

4 or 5 mountain, sand, and nature fabrics: total of ½ yard

Backing for MY CLASS SAMPLE: 1 yard

Backing for THE VEIL IN THE TETONS: 1½ yards

Batting: cut 4" longer and wider than the wallhanging

Binding for MY CLASS SAMPLE: 23" square for bias or straight-grain

Binding for THE VEIL IN THE TETONS: 26" square for bias or straight-grain

## Assembly

**1.** On the grid paper, draw vertical, horizontal, or diagonal lines to divide the picture area into equal divisions. A 2" or 3" wide row works well for these quilts, which have picture areas of about 20" x 30".

*The grid-paper image will be reversed from the finished quilt because the templates are pressed on the backs of the fabrics. You can make a master drawing first, if you like, then reverse the drawing on the grid paper.*

**2.** Use a pencil to sketch the mountains, sand dunes, etc., and draw a line to separate the ground area from the sky in the distance.

*A Flexicurve works well for drawing the curved features of the landscape (see page 55).*

**3.** Then, with an indelible pen and a ruler, replace the curved lines with straight lines within each row (fig. 2–1).

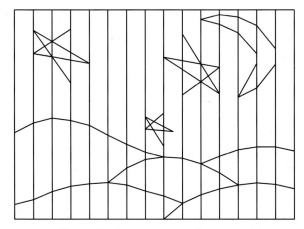

**Fig. 2–1.** Draw MY CLASS SAMPLE on iron-on grid paper, and replace curved lines with straight lines in each vertical row.

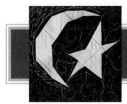

**4.** Create any sky accents, such as stars, moon, birds, or hot air balloons. (For smaller stars, you can divide one vertical row into three sections.) Code each row A, B, etc., then code the templates inside each row A1, A2, A3, and so on.

**5.** Make fabric selections and cut them into strips ½" wider than the drawn grid-paper rows. Cut the paper templates apart, working with just two or three rows at a time. Press the templates onto the backs of the fabric strips, leaving a ¼" seam allowance on each side of the templates. Trim off the extra fabric at each end, leaving a ¼" seam allowance. "Pin and peek" as each new piece is added to the row.

**6.** Once the separate rows have been stitched, the grid on the paper can be used to align the intersections for pinning. For ease in stitching rows together, remove the paper on one side, as follows: Row A templates can be removed so that, on row B, there will be a guide to follow for stitching. Then match the next two rows. Remove templates from row B and use the C templates as a guide, etc.

**7.** Finish with a border. For added interest, you can change the border fabric colors where the land and sky colors change.

## Borders

### MY CLASS SAMPLE

Cut two borders 4½" x 20½" and sew them to the sides of the quilt. Cut two borders 4½" x 38½" and sew them to the top and bottom.

### THE VEIL IN THE TETONS

Use freezer paper to design this striking border. On the freezer paper, draw the top border 6" x 42" with mitered corners. Divide the border into nine angled sections: one center section and four sections on either side. Mix the fabrics for the border to correspond to the inside land fabrics. Cut apart the freezer-paper templates. Press them onto the backs of the fabrics and add a ¼" seam allowance when you cut the fabric pieces, then sew them together. Repeat for the bottom row.

Draw the side border on freezer paper, 6" x 32". Divide the border in half along its length. Each side border was adjusted to meet the mountains and sky on the sides. Repeat the same cut, press, and stitch sequence as before. Add a 4" border around the entire wallhanging, if you like.

NAUSET LIGHT, CAPE COD, 28" x 37", by Marion Corneel of Southern Pines, North Carolina, was made in a class with the author. Marion captures memories of where she grew up on Cape Cod with this strip-pieced beach landscape, complete with lighthouse, sunshine, and sailboat.

# Flexicurve Formula

After years of straight-line piecing, I discovered the Flexicurve. This rubberized, flexible tool retains its shape when bent. It is used for drafting soft curves. The ½" Flexicurve has a built in seam allowance. Whether you mark along the top or the bottom, the actual seam is right in the middle.

I have a simple system for using this tool to make curved fabric sections:

**1.** Bend the Flexicurve to the desired soft curves and situate it on the base (sky) fabric. *Always mark on the right side of the fabric.* Place pins, on both the top and bottom of the Flexicurve, where you want your line to begin and end. Use a chalk roller or a pencil to draw along the bottom edge between these pins. (Think "base-bottom" to remember which side of the Flexicurve you should mark.) Cut on this line (fig. 2–2).

**2.** Choose a new fabric addition (mountain) that is larger than the base fabric. Be sure to match the grain lines of the mountain and sky fabrics. Without changing the bends in the Flexicurve, position it on the mountain fabric, near the top. Draw along the top edge. Where the pins are, draw vertical lines to the top of the fabric piece. Cut on the line, keeping the extensions at both ends (fig. 2–3).

**3.** At the extensions, snip the seam allowances to release them. Place the cut sky and mountain fabrics, right sides together, at each end and pin in place. Machine sew the seam, aligning the raw edges of the curves (fig. 2–4). Be careful not to stretch the fabrics, but ease gently as you sew. Trim the finished piece to the desired size (fig. 2–5).

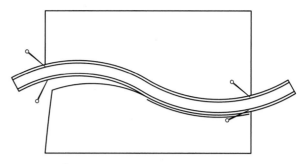

**Fig. 2–2.** Mark the ends of the curves with pins, draw a line along the bottom edge, and cut on the line.

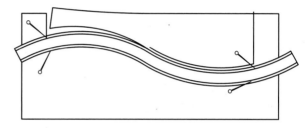

**Fig. 2–3.** Mark the second fabric along the top edge of the Flexicurve and cut on the line.

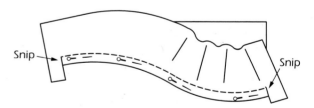

**Fig. 2–4.** Snip the seam allowances at the extensions before sewing.

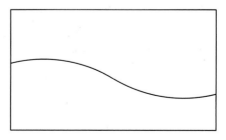

**Fig. 2–5.** Completed curved seam.

## MINI MOUNTAINS IN PLAID
### and
### SURF'S UP

**LEFT:** MINI MOUNTAINS IN PLAID, 35" x 42", by the author.
**OPPOSITE PAGE:** PURPLE MOUNTAIN MAJESTY, 96" x 109", by the author.
**BELOW:** SURF'S UP, 57" x 56", by the author.

**M**y fondness for mountain designs has led me to the diamond shape. The wide, obtuse angle of a 60-degree diamond reflects the gentle mountains or even the sand dunes that characterize landscapes. To make your quilt, try the watercolor approach of using many different prints, but capture the scene in diamonds instead of squares.

The size of the quilt or wallhanging will be determined by the size of the base diamond selected. Try your hand with either a 6", 9", or 12" diamond (patterns on page 62). MINI MOUNTAINS IN PLAID, page 57, is based on a 6" diamond; SURF'S UP, page 57, a 9" diamond; and PURPLE MOUNTAIN MAJESTY, page 56, a 12" diamond.

You may copy the diamond grid on page 61, as needed, to help you plan a simple mountain scene. To add interest to your quilt, the diamonds can be subdivided into Four-Patches or Nine-Patches. For instance, a Four-Patch for the 6" diamond would consist of four 3" diamonds. A Nine-Patch for the 9" diamond would have nine 3" diamonds, but a Four-Patch for the 9" diamond would have four 4½" diamonds. Add stars and a sun or moon, if you like (see Making Diamond Stars, page 59).

Listing the fabric amounts in scrap quilts is a challenge, especially with so many variables, so I will give a generous amount for the sky, plus the star accent for three quilt sizes. Then you may need to rely on your quilt friends to share fabric, so you will have enough different colors and prints for your watercolor landscape.

*It would be really helpful to have a design wall for planning this quilt, and you may want to involve your family and friends in deciding color placement.*

## MATERIALS

| Fabric | Quilt size | Total yards |
|--------|-----------|-------------|
| Sky scraps | Small (6" diamond) | 1 |
| | Medium (9" diamond) | 2½ |
| | Large (12" diamond) | 4½ |
| Star/moon scraps | Small (6" diamond) | ¼ |
| | Medium (9" diamond) | 1 |
| | Large (12" diamond) | 1½ |

## Quilt Assembly

**1.** Copy the diamond grid on page 61. Color in your favorite mountain shades on the copy. This shading will determine how many diamonds will be needed for each color.

**2.** Decide on the size of the quilt you want to make (6", 9", or 12" base diamond). Note the number of sky diamonds and the number of mountain diamonds needed. Audition various shades of green and rust fabrics and play with subdividing the diamonds.

**3.** Make an iron-on grid paper template for each size of diamond from the patterns on page 62. Use the templates to cut your fabric pieces.

**4.** First pin and sew any subdivided diamonds, such as a star, moon, Four-Patch, Nine-Patch, etc. Then piece the diamonds in diagonal rows to finish your quilt top.

## Making Diamond Stars

Stars of different sizes are fun to add to your diamond quilts. Note that the stars will be reversed when using iron-on grid paper.

**1.** Divide a grid-paper diamond into three rows by dividing two opposite sides equally. For instance, a 6" diamond has 2" divisions, a 9" diamond has 3" divisions, and a 12" diamond has 4" divisions. Label the diamond as shown in figure 2–6.

**2.** With pencil and ruler, draw a line from B to D. Then mark a line from D to A. Draw a line from A through the circled intersection back to D. A final line goes to B, but through the C intersection (fig. 2–7).

*One iron-on template can be re-pressed to cut repeated shapes in various prints. If using an iron-on grid paper template, align the fabric grain lines with the grid, adding a ¼" seam allowance to the fabric pieces with a ruler and rotary cutter. If you like, you can make plastic templates which include ¼" seam allowances added on all sides.*

**3.** Code the templates as shown in figure 2–8, page 60, eliminating some lines that were needed for drafting. Cut the paper star apart and press (cotton setting) the templates onto the backs of the fabrics. Cut the fabric pieces with a ¼" seam allowance around all sides.

**4.** Set up the star rows in sequence ready for piecing. "Pin and peek" for each seam allowance to align the grids on the templates. Do not stitch through the paper but sew right next to the edge.

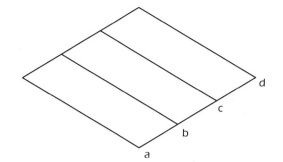

**Fig. 2–6.** Use letters to label the lines.

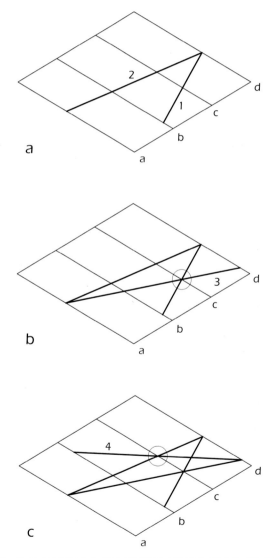

**Fig. 2–7.** Creating a star: (a) Draw lines 1 and 2. (b) Add line 3. (c) Line 4 completes the star.

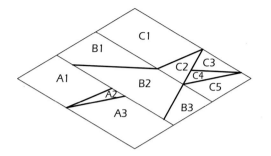

**Fig. 2–8.** Code the pieces before cutting the template apart.

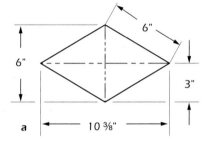

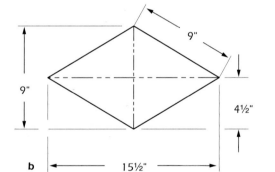

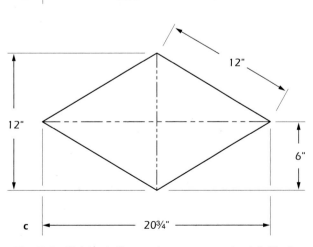

**Fig. 2–9.** Finished diamond measurements: (a) 6" diamond, (b) 9" diamond, (c) 12" diamond.

**5.** After each row has been pieced, sew the three rows together, using the grid paper as a pinning guide. The paper may be removed before stitching. Save the templates because they can be re-ironed many times.

*A moon may be inserted into a diamond by using a Flexicurve (see page 55) to draw the curves.*

## Diamond Measurements

Referring to figure 2–9, use the finished measurements for 6", 9", and 12" diamonds to help you figure the size of your quilt for adding borders.

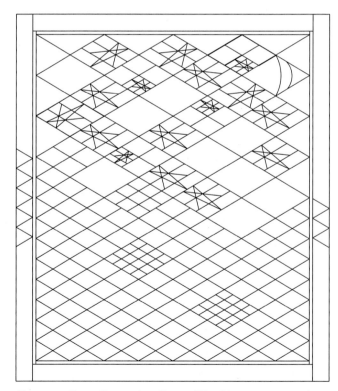

DIAMOND STAR. Example of a quilt with a moon and many stars. Notice how the 60-degree diamonds extend into the border.

# Blank Diamond Grid

This 60-degree diamond grid can be copied as needed for personal use.

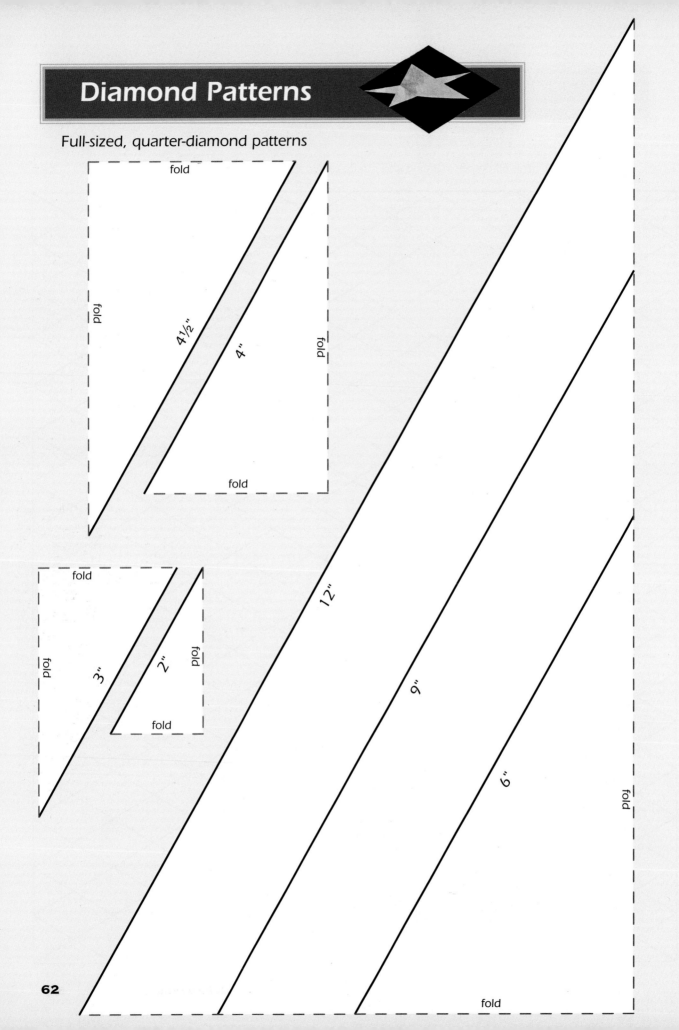

# Diamond Patterns

Full-sized, quarter-diamond patterns

**TOP:** MODA MOUNTAINS FOR THE COMMUNITY FOUNDATION, 29¾" x 33½", by the author. Thread sketching accents an array of Moda solid colors, representing mountains and sky with star accents.

**BOTTOM:** TWO GEESE AND A STAR, 68" x 51", by the author.

**TOP:** BLUE RIDGE MOUNTAINS, 52½" x 37½", made by Gwen Albert.

**BOTTOM:** SYMPHONY SUNSET, 52" x 72", made by the author and owned by Margarite Wilson. Musical notes and fabric highlight a sunset setting in the Smokies. A medley of scrap fabrics echoes the many mountain ranges in this quilt made for the Hendersonville Symphony Orchestra.

# Many Mountains Variation

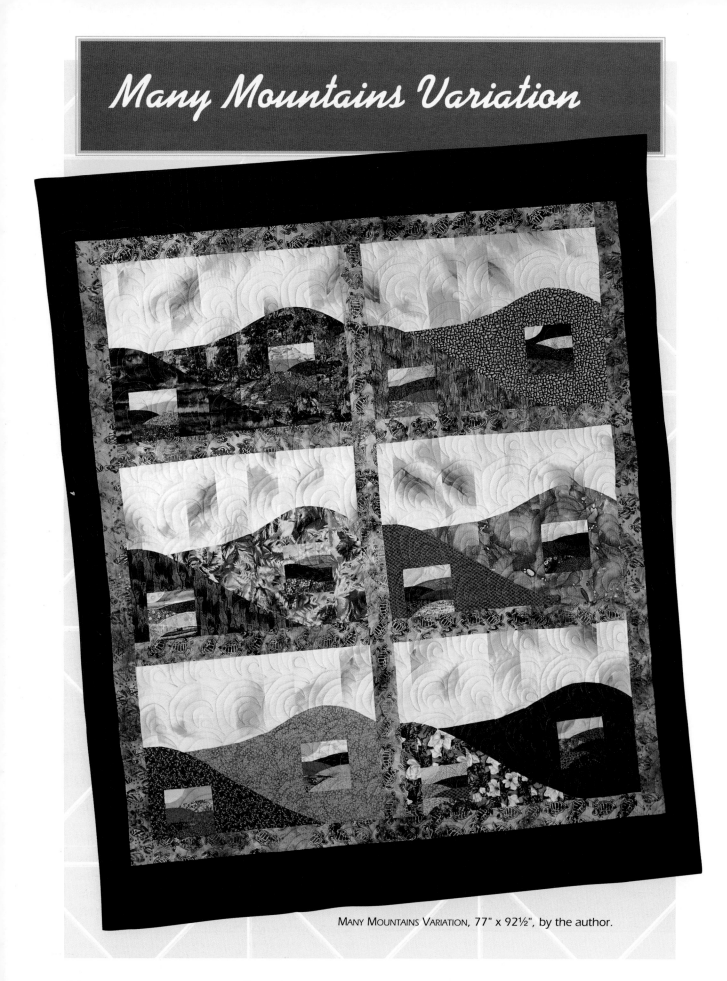

MANY MOUNTAINS VARIATION, 77" x 92½", by the author.

# Many Mountains Variation

## MANY MOUNTAINS VARIATION, 77" x 92½"

### MATERIALS

Sky fabric: 2 yards

Mountain fabric: 12 different fat quarters 18" x 22"

12 completed Many Mountains blocks from the COUNTRY TO COUNTRY SAMPLER, page 48.

*Try an exchange with a group of friends: make the same mountain 12 times, same fabric, then exchange blocks for a glorious surprise.*

Sashing: 1 yard

Inner border: 1 yard

Outside border: 2⅞ yards

Batting: 81" x 97"

Backing: 5½ yards

Binding: ¾ yard

Iron-on grid paper: 21½" x 30"

## Cutting

### Sashing

Cut 4 strips 3½" x 30½".

Cut 3 strips 3½" x 24". Piece to make one long strip. Trim to 71".

### Inner border

Cut 4 strips 3½" x 33". Piece to make two long strips. Trim both to 63½".

Cut 4 strips 3½" x 39". Piece to make two long strips. Trim both to 77".

### Outside border

Cut 2 strips 8½" x 69½" (parallel to selvages)
Cut 2 strips 4½" x 93" (parallel to selvages)

## Quilt Assembly

**1.** Divide the grid paper sheet into vertical rows with at least two rows having a 6" span for the Many Mountains blocks. Create two mountains by drawing gentle curves with a pencil (fig. 2–10).

BELOW: **Fig. 2–10.** Example of grid-paper drawing.

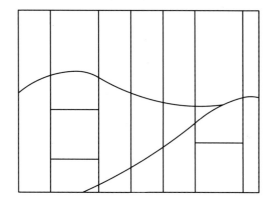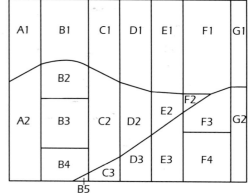

**2.** "Correct" each curved pencil line, in between the vertical lines, by replacing it with a straight line. Keep the wider curves that are easy to piece. (All of this drawing is done without seam allowances.)

**3.** Code the grid template by assigning a letter to each row and a number to each piece within the row. Code, or use a colored pencil, to indicate the two different mountains. Mark where the 6" Many Mountains blocks will be placed.

**4.** Cut the vertical rows apart. Separate out all the sky templates. Cut the sky fabric pieces ½" wider than the templates. Press each

sky template on the back of the fabric, leaving a ¼" seam allowance on each side of the template. Trim the seam allowance off at each end, leaving a ¼" seam allowance. Cut five more fabrics for each sky template.

**5.** Separate the two mountain templates. Repeat the same cutting steps as for the sky. Make six different blocks, using contrasting fabrics for the two mountains, but with the same templates.

**6.** Sew the pieces together into rows, including the 6" Many Mountains blocks, then sew the rows together. Note how the design is reversed because the templates were pressed to the backs of the fabrics. The blocks should measure 22" x 30½" on the raw edges.

*For sewing the rows together, align the grids on the templates. Pin and peek! As the rows are matched and pinned, remove the templates on the underside before sewing the seams. Keep the templates stored in an envelope well marked for quilt name and block size.*

**7.** Sew the 30½" sashings between the blocks, as shown in figure 2–11. Connect the mountain blocks with the 71" center sashing strip.

**8.** Add the 33" inner border strips to the top and bottom, then add the side borders. Sew the 8½" wide outer borders on the top and bottom, finishing with the 4½" side borders.

**9.** Layer the backing, batting, and quilt top, and quilt the layers. Quilting was done on a longarm quilting machine, with variegated threads and an arc design.

**Fig. 2–11.** Quilt assembly.

# Chapter 3

# Get-Real Garments

Once you have covered the beds and the walls with quilts, it is only natural to consider your body. Hence, quilted fashions have found a place in our quilt world.

My fashion history is similar to many: paper dolls (remember Brenda Starr?), doll clothes, home economics classes (using a pedal sewing machine), and finally the fashion office at Marshall Field & Co. Imagine getting to pull garments and accessories from all over the store to dress the store window mannequins. It was my first job out of college! Then I was promoted to real models for their glamorous fashion shows. So I have always loved clothes and somehow equated looking good in a new outfit to having a good time. A new party dress meant being the belle of the ball.

As my quilting career developed, making quilted garments became an additional focus. The Fairfield Processing Fashion Show, now the Bernina® of America Fashion Show, have certainly opened our eyes to the patchwork possibilities for clothing. At first, every garment I made was hand quilted, but soon I realized that fashions change (and so does our body shape) so machine quilting was more realistic.

You can trace this fashion history through the years by gazing at my period vests and jackets on pages 88–89. Certain vests became

a.

b.

String vest with irregular widths sewn and flipped from a triangle: (a) back, (b) front.

classics, and there are ones I would wear repeatedly, like my postage stamp vest. Why, I made it in three different color variations. The true test of any garment is whether it can be worn socially with non-quilting people. More often, we are more comfortable wearing such clothing with guild members or at a quilt convention.

I recall a particular incident related to clothes. Soon after the release of the first fabric collection I designed, I found myself wondering what to do with all of the selvage strips. I finally decided to stitch 6" lengths of them on a recycled denim jacket.

To give each strip weight, I attached a bead at the end. My mother was a good assistant during this period, so she helped with this time-consuming task. However, she inadvertently made a mistake by placing the tiny crochet hook we were using next to my dad's

Crazy patch goes down and denim.

chair. He thought it was a toothpick and soon exclaimed, "Virginia, take me to the emergency room!" Fortunately, it was easily removed.

Remember that quilt I was working on in the hospital? After it was finished, I went one step further and made an outfit to match the quilt. Now, all I have left is the outfit. It seems our local congressman admired my quilt and asked that it be hung in his Washington, D.C., office. Of course, I was flattered, so I loaned it out for several months. It was returned, but then I had a big favor to ask of him. Right before I was to leave on an international quilt trip, I could not find my passport. We looked in all the right places, to no avail. What do you do but call your congressman for help. He tried all weekend to make the right arrangements, but it was hopeless. With much stress, I continued to pack my bags. The morning I was to leave, another person searched the drawer where it was supposed to be and voila, there it was! Once I returned from the trip, the only thing I could do was give the quilt to my congressman for all his efforts. That is how I lost my LIBERTY quilt, but you can be sure I have not misplaced my passport anymore.

Now, as a new generation emerges in our family, I can focus my quilting knowledge onto my grandchildren. The same garment-making methods that apply to adults work well for children, just on a smaller scale. For your quilted garments, you can explore strip piecing, sew-and-flip, weaving, and crazy-patch methods. Having a color theme is the secret to a definitive quilted garment.

# Weave a Wonder

Child's vest.

Adult's vest.

It does not get much simpler than weaving to create a dynamic effect for a vest. Discover the serendipity in the process of making the adult- or child-sized woven vests. These pieces were made with leftover fabric colored with Setacolor paints. With the paints somewhat diluted, wonderful pastel shades occur.

### MATERIALS

**Adult or child vest pattern, with no darts**

Vest lining for the back and two front pieces

Lightweight fusible web the same size

**Adult vest:** 4 fabric squares 24" x 24" (or paint, with Setacolor, 4 muslin 24" squares). Cut the squares into 24 bias strips 1" wide for weaving. Some piecing of bias strips is required.

23 random buttons

**Child vest:** 4 fabric squares 16" x 16". Cut the squares into 18 bias strips 1" wide.

Buttons

## Assembly

**1.** Follow the pattern to cut the front and back vest pieces from the lining fabric and the fusible web.

**2.** Stitch the lining shoulder seams together. Trim off the seam allowance on the fusible web to butt the vest shoulder seams together. Gently remove the paper backing from the fusible or follow the manufacturer's directions.

**3.** Spread the lining piece, wrong side up, on a large cutting mat and place the web piece, fusible side down, on the lining.

**4.** Using the 45-degree line of a rotary ruler and a pencil, lightly draw a few diagonal guidelines on the fusible web. Following your guidelines and starting on the back of the vest, place fabric strips next to each other, all on the same diagonal (fig. 3–1). Pin the ends in place.

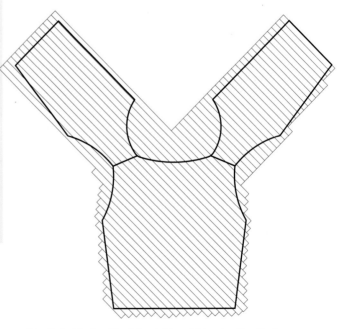

**Fig. 3–1.** Vest with strips laid out in one direction.

**5.** Once the web is covered on one diagonal, weave strips on the other diagonal, again starting on the back (fig. 3–2). Continue the weaving over the vest fronts. Notice that, as the strips come over to the front of the vest, they naturally end up aligned vertically and horizontally rather than diagonally – hence the serendipity!

**6.** Continue weaving until the fusible web is completely covered. Trim off the fabric strips at the pattern edge. Using a pressing cloth, press the entire vest with an iron set on cotton. Quilt the raw edges every other row with variegated thread and a machine feather stitch. The vest edges can be bound or finished with a zigzag stitch.

Here is a fun finishing idea. If you leave the horizontal strips from the front pieces untrimmed at the side seams, you can overlap them to the back, securing them with random buttons and letting the ends hang loose for about 1".

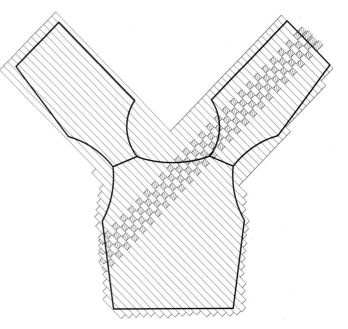

**Fig. 3–2.** Weave strips on the other diagonal.

A fun side-seam treatment.

# Tumbling Blocks or Star?

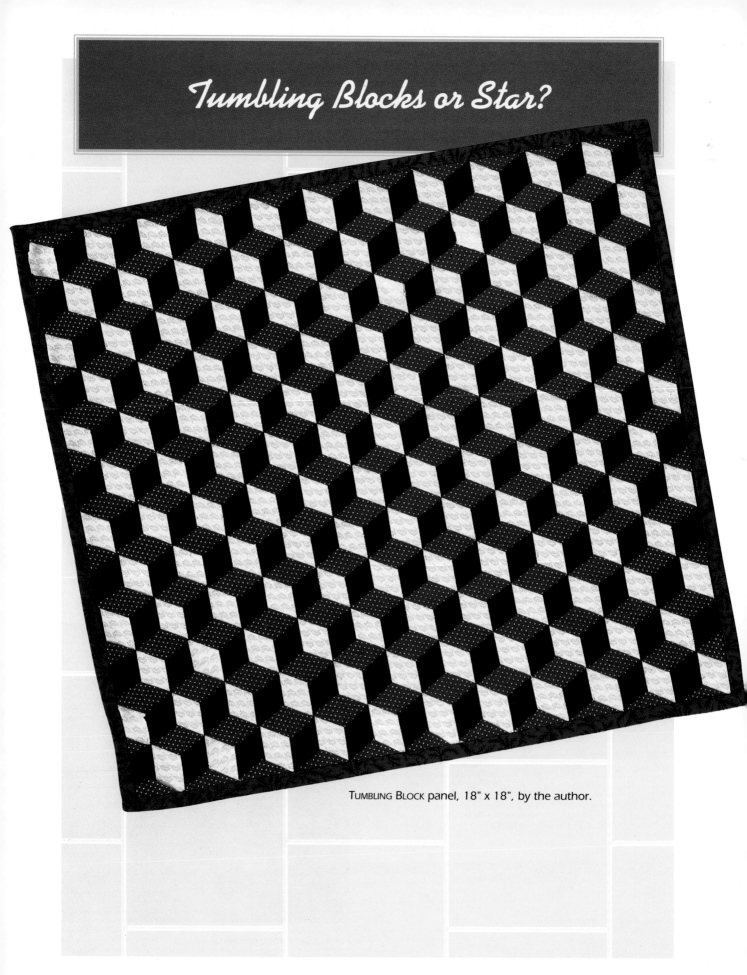

TUMBLING BLOCK panel, 18" x 18", by the author.

Just what do you see when you gaze at this 60-degree design? Your eyes play a game deciding the interplay of the three colors. Once again, the use of bias strips makes this method akin to ribbon weaving, but much more reasonable and available because of our "quilters' stashes." While I was teaching at the John C. Campbell Folk School (Brasstown, North Carolina) recently, a basket maker noted that this weaving has a name in her craft world, "triaxial weaving."

**Quilt size: 18" x 18"**

## MATERIALS

18" bias-cut (on-point) square of light fabric for the vertical strips (warp)
*Note: Using a bias-cut square will produce bias strips of equal length.*

20" square of backing or foundation fabric

18" square of lightweight fusible

20" squares of two fabrics: bright and dark

Binding: 2¼ yards

Serger tweezers

Pins

## Assembly

**1.** Place the backing fabric, wrong side up, on a cutting or flannel board that will hold pins. Center the fusible square on top, allowing 1" on all sides. After the fusible is centered, gently remove the paper.

**2.** Cut vertical strips every ¾" apart out of the bias-cut 18" square. This makes 24 strips. Arrange these strips, right side up, next to each other on the backing fabric and on top of the fusible. Anchor each end with pins (fig. 3–3, page 74).

**3.** Stack the bright and dark 20" squares together (with the bright on top) and cut them into ¾" bias strips (45-degree diagonal). Do not move these strips in preparation for weaving.

*If using a stripe, check, or plaid, cut the strips on a 60-degree angle because the weaving creates 60-degree diamonds.*

### FIRST WEAVING

**4.** Using the 60-degree angle line of your rotary ruler, mark a diagonal guide line on the fusible, starting near the upper-left corner of the pinned strips, with chalk or disappearing pen. Select a bias-cut bright strip that corresponds to the drawn line length.

**5.** Start weaving at the drawn line, working from left to right and down toward the right side (fig. 3–3, page 74). Label the rows, 1, 2, 3, etc., on the left as you commence the weaving process.

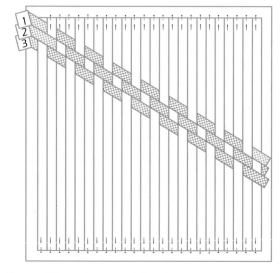

**Fig. 3–3.** Weave from top left to bottom right.

*Always select bias strips that correspond to the desired length. Be sure to butt the long, raw edges next to each other for a compact weaving.*

Weave three repeating rows, as follows:

**1st row:** over 1 (first time only), under 1, over 2 to the end.

**2nd row:** over 2, under 1 to the end.

**3rd row:** under 1, over 2 to the end.

To complete the first weaving, weave upward from the guide line, reversing the sequence of the rows; that is, row 3, row 2, row 1 (fig. 3–5). Sometimes, it is necessary to unpin and use the serger tweezers to ease the weaving process.

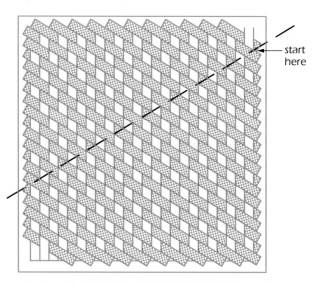

**Fig. 3–4.** Observe the starting point for the second weaving.

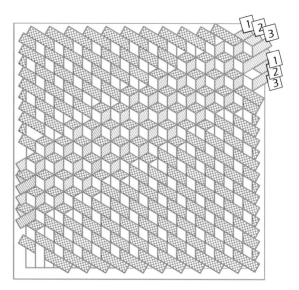

**Fig. 3–5.** Completed weaving.

## SECOND WEAVING

**6.** Using the 60-degree-angle line of your rotary ruler, mark a guide line, starting near the upper-right corner, where indicated in figure 3–4, page 74. This line will split the first light diamond where a dark strip will weave underneath.

**7.** Pick up a corresponding dark bias strip and begin weaving at the starting point.

Weave three repeating rows, as follows:

**1st row:** over 1, under 2 to the end.

**2nd row:** under 1 (first time only), over 1, under 2 to the end.

**3rd row:** under 2, over 1 to the end.

Complete the weaving to the bottom of the quilt, then reverse the steps going upward: row 3, row 2, row 1 (fig. 3–5, page 74). Trim any excess fabric around the 18" square, baste, and press with a warm iron (cotton setting with a press cloth). Bind the raw edges and use the piece as a wallhanging, pillow top, or vest front. I chose to make a button bib front for a western shirt. It was part of my wardrobe for my last television series.

Georgia's shirt with woven bib.

Sew-and-Flip Vest. This vest was made for the author's granddaughter, Claire.

Adult Strip-Star Jacket. The adult jacket is based on an extra-large navy sweatshirt.

## Gram Gram's Collection

Star-Studded Strip Pieced. An array of patriotic fabrics decorates Georgia's jacket.

Child's Meow Jacket. A cat was included in the crazy patch on one front of the jacket. The letters "MEOW" were stitched in the sleeves.

Anna's Wavy-Strips Jacket with hood: (a) front, (b) back.

b.

a.

The Denim "Off" Jacket for Jonah.

M y Americana collection is repre-
sentative of our favorite patchwork techniques. What sets
these apart is their patriotic color scheme. In
each garment, I rely on over-the-counter, easy
children's patterns. Batting varies depending
on the climate in the grandchild's area. It is
smart to choose a lining that makes it easy for
little hands and arms to navigate.

## String Piecing

### Sew-and-Flip vest

Granddaughter Claire's vest (shown on
page 76) was made with the sew-and-flip technique. The strips are built on a right-angle triangle at the bottom of each front piece and
the center back.

### MATERIALS

**Small vest pattern without darts**

Scraps of navy and red

Appropriate lining

Batting or foundation fabric

12" separating zipper (or size required
by your pattern)

## Assembly

**1.** Cut the vest back and front pieces
from the batting or foundation fabric.

**2.** Cut random red and navy fabric pieces
into 2" wide strips. Join several red strips, with
45-degree diagonal seams to make one strip
three yards long. Repeat for the blue strips.

**3.** Cut a 5½" square twice diagonally to
make quarter-square triangles. Center and pin
one of the triangles to the bottom edge of the
back foundation piece and one triangle to each
front piece. There will be one extra triangle.

**4.** Sew and flip the 2" strips to the batting or foundation (fig. 3–6, page 79). Balance
the colors on each side so they alternate red,
blue, red, etc. Finger-press each strip before
adding the next one. Continue adding strips to
cover the foundations. Trim the fabric strips
even with the edges of the foundations.

**5.** Stitch the shoulder seams together, then
the lining shoulder seams. Add a faced neck-
band. With a zipper foot, attach the separating
zipper. With right sides together, attach the lining to the neck, front, and armholes, leaving the
sides open for turning. Turn the vest right side
out. Machine stitch the side seams. Complete by
hand stitching the side lining seams.

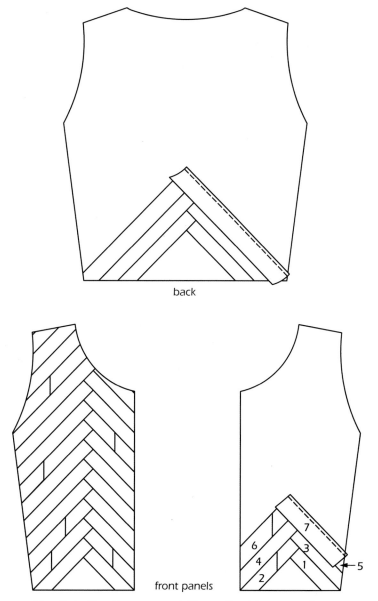

back

front panels

**Fig. 3–6.** Use the sew-and-flip method to cover the foundation pieces.

# Strip Piecing

## Child's Jacket

Star-Studded Strip Pieced. An array of patriotic fabrics decorates a child's jacket (shown on page 76) .

### MATERIALS

**Easy child's jacket pattern without darts**

Foundation and lining

4 to 5 patriotic fabrics in half-yard lengths

Iron-on grid paper

12" separating zipper (or size required by your pattern)

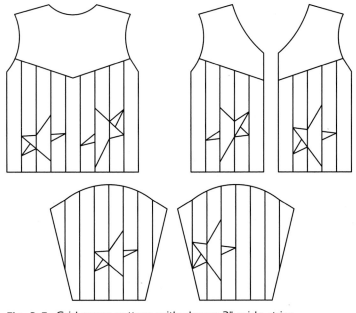

**Fig. 3–7.** Grid-paper pattern with drawn 2" wide strips and added stars.

## Assembly

**1.** Transfer each pattern piece, including the sleeves but not the yoke, to the iron-on grid paper, matching the grain lines with the grid. Divide the grid pattern into vertical strips according to the pattern size: the child's version has 2" wide strips (fig. 3–7).

**2.** Referring to Making Diamond Stars on page 59, draw your stars on the grid-paper pieces, where desired, and code the stars as described. Cut all the grid strip pieces apart to use as templates.

**3.** Cut fabric strips ½" wider than the drawn strips. Press the templates onto the backs of the appropriate fabric strips. Trim the fabric strips ¼" above and below each template, for seam allowances. Stitch the strip and star pieces together one strip at a time. Then sew the strips together to complete each jacket piece. Use the gridded paper template as a pinning guide for the rows, but remove the underneath (feed-dog side) templates before stitching.

*Note that the pattern, once stitched, will be reversed from the grid drawing.*

**4.** Stack each sewn piece with batting and lining and quilt the layers. Machine stitch in the ditch and quilt angles to echo the star lines.

**5.** You can use a sewing machine or a serger to join the shoulders and sides and to inset the sleeves. Complete the raw edges with binding.

## Adult's Jacket

Adult Strip-Star Jacket (page 76). The adult jacket is based on an extra-large navy sweatshirt.

For the adult jacket, you will need five to six patriotic fabrics in half-yard lengths. Follow the instructions for making the child's jacket, but use strips that are 3" wide (fig. 3–8).

This jacket is based on a cut-apart navy sweatshirt. The shoulders were opened, after removing the ribbing and the sleeves, to provide a flat surface for applying the pieced strips. Note the offset front cut instead of a center cut. The strips are separated from the yoke area with a silver bias-strip trim, cut 1" wide. The binding was cut 2" wide, and it was applied to the raw edges with a serpentine stitch.

## Strip-Piecing Variation

An alternate strip-pieced child's jacket or vest has wavy rows (page 77). Use a Flexicurve to make a repeat curved pattern for the seams or use the full-sized wavy-strip pattern on page 82 (fig. 3–9).

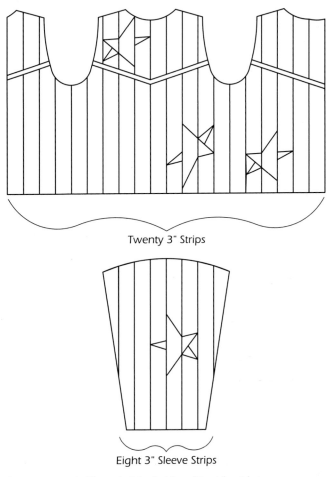

Twenty 3" Strips

Eight 3" Sleeve Strips

**Fig. 3–8.** The adult jacket has 3" wide strips.

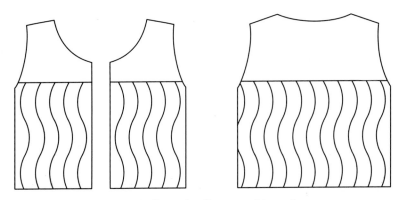

**Fig. 3–9.** Example of a wavy-strip vest.

# FULL-SIZED WAVY-STRIP PATTERN

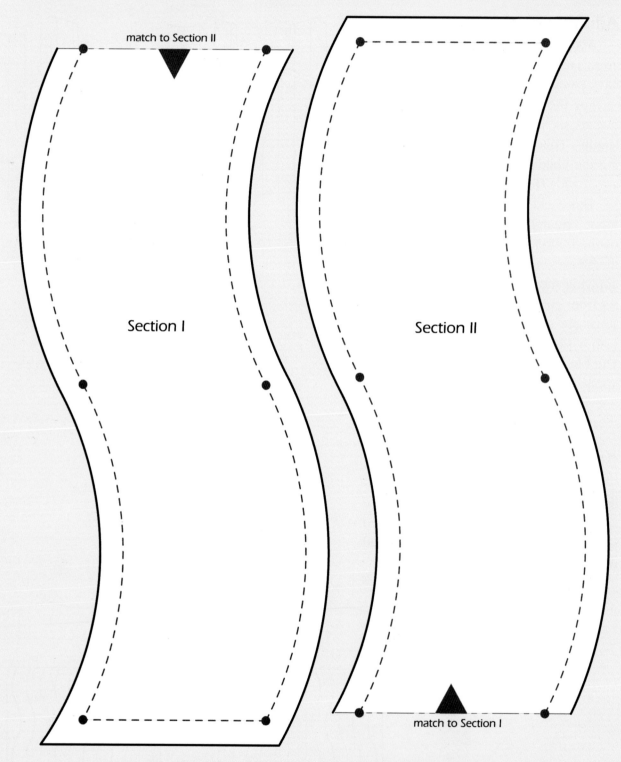

match to Section II

Section I

Section II

match to Section I

Join the two pieces at the "notch" for a 2" wide, 14" long strip.

## Crazy-Patch Study

Child's Meow Jacket (page 77). A cat was included in the crazy patch on one front of the jacket. The letters "MEOW" were drawn on the sleeves.

Crazy patch is as old as the hills, but it's always one of my favorites. It adapts to hand-bags, quilts, and garments. I use the same two crazy-patch methods, planned and unplanned, for making a jacket as presented for the hand-bags described on pages 15–20.

In theory, it may seem easy to stitch random scraps together, but in practice, it takes a good eye to arrange the pieces so they fit together well. Consider the balance of light and dark, the size of each piece, and the introduction of a geometric print, like a check or plaid.

### MATERIALS

**Child's jacket pattern, without darts, with foundation and lining; or child's vest pattern with lining**

Scraps of patriotic fabrics with a good contrast. For the denim vest, the use of worn-out blue jeans combines well with calicos and plaid fabric.

Batting is not required with heavier denim.

Iron-on grid paper

12" separating zippers for each project (or size required for pattern)

## Assembly

**1.** For the planned crazy-patch version, transfer the jacket or vest pattern to iron-on grid paper and create random lines of about the same length for the crazy-patch seams.

*If the pattern is to be pressed on the fabric backs, then draw any letters or motifs in reverse.*

**2.** Code the jacket sections as described on page 84 (fig. 3-10). Cut apart the grid-paper pieces to use as templates for cutting fabric pieces. Use an iron, on the cotton setting, to press the templates onto the backs of the appropriate fabric pieces.

**3.** Cut the fabric pieces out, adding ¼" seam allowances with a rotary cutter and ruler. Sew the crazy-patch pieces together.

**4.** After each jacket piece has been stitched, layer it with lightweight batting and lining and quilt the layers.

*With the Meow jacket, I used my walking foot to cover the seams with a variegated serpentine machine stitch. With denim overlapping the raw edges, it works well to use decorative stitches and a bobbin thread that matches the lining. Plaid binding accents this vest.*

**5.** Assemble the jacket pieces with a serger and bind any raw edges.

*To sew the jacket pieces together, align the paper edges and pin. Then pull off the paper before stitching the jacket seams.*

The "Off" jacket on page 77 has a story. With much pride, our grandson, Jonah W. Bonesteel, was invited to appear as a guest on the opening of my "Garment Show" on television. Being only 2 years old, he had hardly spoken any words, so all I hoped for was a smile. He walked on the brightly lit set and tried the jacket on easily enough. In the flag pockets I had placed some goodies for him to examine. After he looked at the pocket goodies, I asked him, "Jonah, do you want to wear your jacket home?" He loudly answered, "Off!"

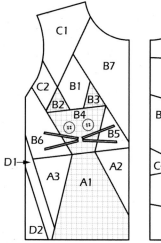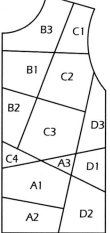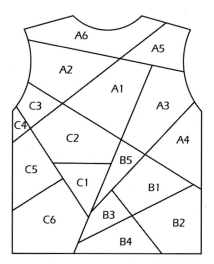

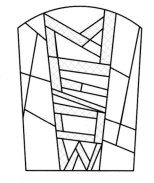

**Fig. 3–10.** Example of planned crazy-patch vest with cat on front and "MEOW" on sleeve.

# Inch by Inch Vests

**Q**uite often, the leftovers from one project can lead to an entirely new project. "Waste not, want not" is a quilter's motto. After I had made a Postage Stamp quilt and then a wallhanging for the Hendersonville City Hall, there was still an abundance of 1" squares, which made a great jacket.

For your inch by inch project, follow the simple vest setting with squared off shoulders for a great vest. The size given is a medium. For a small, take fuller seam allowances. Note the alternate size given for the full figure.

## MATERIALS

380 or so 1½" squares, creating a scrappy look in a color theme (have a "postage stamp" party with your groupies)

2 sets of dark and light strips cut 1½" x 36" for the front and back diamonds

3 strips 1½" x 9½", inside the diamonds

4 strips 1½" x 7½", inside the diamonds

4 strips 1½" x 5½", inside the diamonds

4 strips 1½" x 3½", inside the diamonds

Lining and batting: cut 22" x 50" for a large and 20" x 42" for medium and small

5 to 7 buttons

Binding: 4½ yards cut 2¼"

Inch by Inch vests.

## Assembly

**1.** Stitch the dark and light 36" strips together in pairs (strip-sets). Cut the strip-sets apart every 1½" and press seam allowances toward the dark side.

**2.** Position the strips for the back and front of the vest, according to the setting diagram (fig. 3–11).

**3.** Place the postage stamp squares on the back, fronts, and sides in vertical rows (fig. 3–12).

**4.** Pin each row and sew the rows together, starting in the back. (Alternate seam allowance direction for ease in piecework.) At the underarm area, sew a slightly wider seam toward the waist to taper the vest slightly (fig. 3–13).

**5.** Layer the batting and lining, and quilt diagonal stitching through the squares, every other row, leaving the shoulder seams open. Accent stitching for the long strips can be decorative or in the ditch. Sew the shoulder seams together with a flat, lapped seam or cover with binding. Binding and buttons complete the vest.

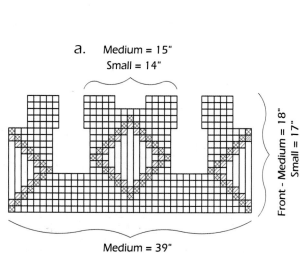

a. Medium = 15"
Small = 14"

Front - Medium = 18"
Small = 17"

Medium = 39"
Small = 37"

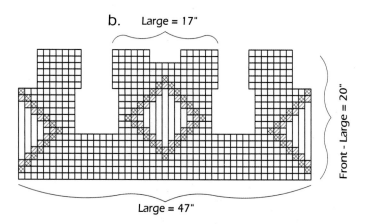

b. Large = 17"

Front - Large = 20"

Large = 47"

**Fig. 3–11.** Setting: (a) small and medium sizes, (b) large size.

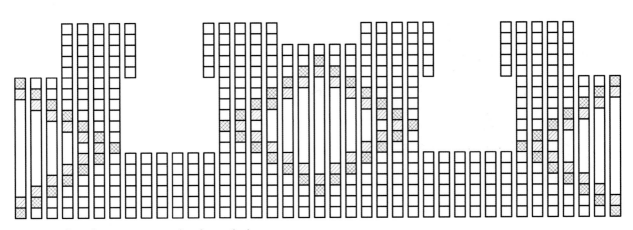

**Fig. 3–12.** Sew the squares together in vertical rows.

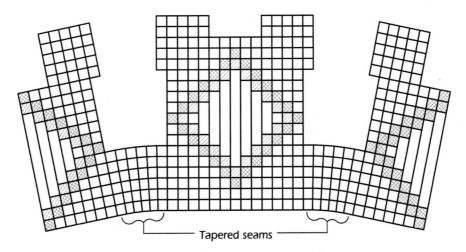

Tapered seams

**Fig. 3–13.** Taper the side seams at the waist.

# A Gallery of Garments

These garments, made by the author, are meant to inspire. For your own quilted clothing, select traditional, commercial patterns, but without any darts.

**LEFT:** This Seminole jacket is accented with ribbon and braid stitched over raw edges.

**BELOW LEFT:** Denim crazy-patch vest.

**BELOW RIGHT:** Silk crazy-patch vest.

**ABOVE LEFT:** Wool strip vest.

**ABOVE RIGHT:** This vest was made at the very first Jinny Beyer Hilton Head Symposium in 1981.

**RIGHT:** Compass blocks give direction to a fun fabric.

# Chapter 4

# *Freedom Escapees*

The joy of quilting has meant so much to so many people individually, and even more so in a group situation. What better way to spend time than learning and sharing a craft together. Quiltmaking has become the vehicle for social interaction while reaping a fabric benefit in the end. I often feel sorry for my non-sewing friends. I actually know people who pay to have their clothes altered! "Learn to sew," has always been my motto.

For more than 30 years, I have been fortunate enough to become a groupie. As founding president of The Western North Carolina Quilt Guild and member of The Landrum Quilt Guild and The Asheville Quilt Guild, I have grown in my field. Then there are the satellite offspring of these groups, such as The Cover Lovers. Quilts in our area were often referred to as "kivers" but we knew we could not call our group Kiver Livers, so the name naturally evolved into Cover Lovers because we are true lovers of all covers.

This group met and bonded in a vest class held in my small studio. It was conducted through Blue Ridge Community College. We were squeezed in with not much visibility when I demonstrated at the sewing machine, but this group clicked. I recall students sitting on my

circular staircase. They came for different reasons from diverse backgrounds, but had a common denominator in quilting. One student came to learn how to stitch the hides she had just tanned. Others were at a mid-life period when quilting was the perfect craft to pursue. Meeting twice monthly since 1981 has resulted in a sisterhood of support. We have lived through parental concerns, husband health situations, divorces of children, and aging situations that have led to older care facilities and surgeries. I will always recall the festive caroling outside my door when I was recovering from my brain surgery. Yes, there is more to making a quilt than to keep warm. There are the social benefits that are long lasting.

When it comes to teaching and groupies, nothing is greater than my Freedom Escape's 20 students. Over 19 years, classes have commenced every winter for a week, set in a lodge nestled in the mountains of western North Carolina. When describing these extensive years of classes, a gentleman in the audience commented, "And they haven't learned yet?" What he did not realize is that every year meant a new project. In this chapter, I present four of the more recent quilts made in our week-long class. In each instance, instruction was given ahead of time so everyone came

# and Beyond . . .

somewhat prepared. Imagine having a full week to stitch at your own sewing station, free of cooking, laundry, and other mundane home chores. It has been a dream come true for these loyal, hard-working quilters. They come from different guilds bringing updated knowledge that we all share. The fact that they try to outwit the teacher and are full of pranks does not deter my objective to finish a quilt. However, sometimes it is not until the next year that we see the results.

One of my favorite classes was the photo-transfer year. Because the supply list included bringing family pictures, I expanded our studies by having everyone tell their family history. This included their heritage, their travels, and their various homes, along with many trials and tribulations. That year we really got to know each other. One time, a pair of ladies nylon bloomers was left in one of the rooms. A "lovely" handbag was made out of them with stuff stitched on all sides, and it was presented to a deserving member. Great idea until someone carried it in town, claiming it was a Bonesteel creation. We soon retired this yearly tacky presentation in an attempt to be more mature. Look carefully on the YOU HAD TO BE THERE quilt (page 92) and you can find the bloomers along with my calculator card.

Speaking of calculators, I have done my best to open the door to math as it pertains to patchwork, but sometimes to no avail. Michael Haun, general manager at the lodge, alias Director of Loose Ends, picked up on my attempt with this fun parody.

**Math Comprehension Test.** The duchess of Windsboro wanted a new quilt, sending out a decree to all the quiltmakers in the land. She enclosed the notice of an award for any quiltmaker being able to piece together these simple directions. Taking the hypotenuse of the sum of the sides of the smallest quilt piece, and adding this to the logarithm of the reciprocal of the needle size, multiply this by the height of the tallest trapunto, if any are used; if not, add the weight of the batting and the length of the thread doubled. This simple formula should give you the outside perimeter of the edging.

Now, without referring to the *previous* paragraph answer these simple questions:
1. What color was the queen's quilt?
2. Did the butler do it?
3. Was the duchess beyond her borders?

You Had to Be There, 57" x 74", by the author.

# Show and Tell Pillow

How many times have you tried to tell a story or relate a wonderful experience when you finally have to admit, "You had to be there." Well, I wish you were all there to share the fun in learning and sharing patchwork at Freedom Escape. Every year I attempt to challenge the students by introducing a new project. We have tried it all! For our eighteenth year of classes, I wanted something really different. It all culminated in this "out of the box" folk-art wallhanging. Ed Larson, a folk artist from Santa Fe, New Mexico, certainly fulfilled my request with this delightful design. I cannot expect everyone to eagerly make this wallhanging, but featuring the "show and tell" ladies makes a great pillow.

## Show and Tell Pillow

**Size: 23" x 23"**

### MATERIALS

Background: 17" x 17"

Assorted scraps: face and hand neutral fabric

Inside accent border: ¼ yard (cut 2 strips 1½" x 16½" and 2 strips 1½" x 18½")

Outside border : ½ yard (cut 2 strips 3" x 18½", cut 2 strips 3" x 23½")

Backing: 23½" x 23½"

Pocket back: cut 2 squares 23½" x 23½"

Pillow form: 16" x 16"

Iron-on grid paper

Batting: 19" x 19"

5 buttons

SHOW AND TELL PILLOW, 23" x23", by the author.

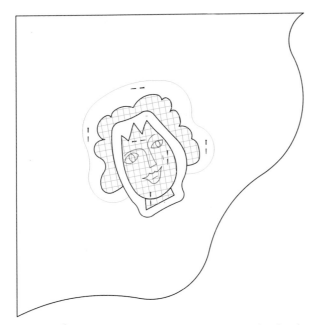

Fig. 4–1. Position the head and hair on the background.

## Pillow Top Assembly

**1.** Transfer Suzy Show and Tilly Tell designs (pages 97–98) onto iron-on grid paper and number the templates.

**2.** Cut the templates and press them (cotton setting) onto the right sides of your chosen fabrics, being careful to align the fabric grain line with the paper grid. Note that template 1 includes the neck. Satin stitching will define the chin.

**3.** Cut the fabric pieces, leaving at least a ¼" allowance around each figure. Leave the paper templates on the fabric pieces. Align the head (piece 1) and hair (piece 2) on the 17" background square (fig. 4–1). Decide on a thread choice for stitching around the figures.

*Black thread will accent each piece and save on changing bobbins to match different colors of top thread.*

*A light box will help in positioning the pieces on the background: Trace the whole design on tracing paper and place the tracing on a light box. Set the background piece on top of the traced design. You should be able to see the design through the background so you can place your appliqué pieces easily.*

**4.** Remove the grid paper from the hair and straight stitch around the face, right next to the paper template. Use lip appliqué scissors to remove excess fabric up to the stitching line, with the template in place (fig. 4–2). Then remove the template.

trim

Fig. 4–2. Straight stitch around the face and neck, then trim away the excess fabric close to the stitching.

**5.** The straight stitches are to be covered with satin stitching. Make a test sample of the stitching first to check for the proper stitch width and length. Place a stabilizer underneath the foundation in the area to be satin stitched, then satin stitch over the straight stitching (fig. 4–3).

*The satin stitching should cover the straight line stitching with the needle going into both the foundation and the face, plus creating the chin.*

**6.** Re-press template 2 onto the hair. Straight stitch around hair, trim away the extra fabric as before, and satin stitch around the hair. Then remove the template as before (fig. 4–4). Continue in the same manner to add the remaining appliqués.

**7.** Make small quilts or use preprinted fabric quilts to fit between the hands. You can put a backing on the quilts so they can hang free, if you like. You may even want to put a few quilting stitches in each quilt.

**8.** Once the figures are secure, you can cut away the foundation underneath the satin-stitched appliqués. Complete with satin-stitched facial features. Trim pillow to 16½" square.

**9.** Add borders with butted or mitered corners, then press.

**Fig. 4–3.** Satin stitch over the straight stitching.

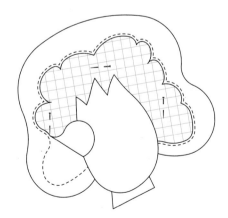

**Fig. 4–4.** Template being removed from straight-stitched hair.

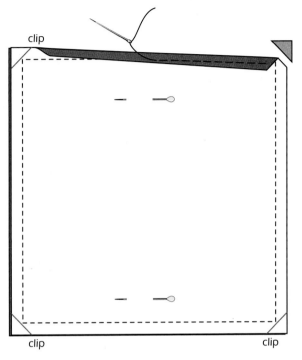

clip

clip          clip

**Fig. 4–5.** Trim the corners.

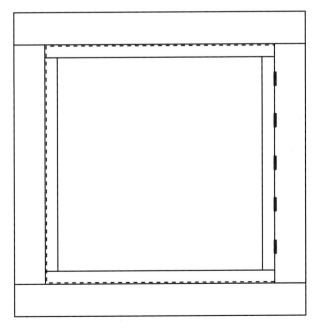

**Fig. 4–6.** Make buttonholes in the border seam.

## Pillow-Form Pocket

Here is a unique and fun way to create a pillow-form pocket for your pillow.

**1.** Cut a piece of batting 19" square and baste it under the center portion of the pillow top.

**2.** Layer the pillow top with the 23½" backing square. Baste and sew the layers together with a ¼" seam allowance, leaving an opening to turn the pillow right side out. Trim the edges and snip off the right-angle corners (fig. 4–5). Whipstitch the opening shut. Quilt the three layers with hand or machine stitching.

**3.** Prepare the separate backing of two 23½" fabrics in the same manner as the front sections.

*Before turning the pillow right side out, baste a ¼" seam allowance on each side of the opening. These basting stitches will make it easier to hand stitch the opening shut after the piece has been turned.*

**4.** Make five buttonholes in the outside border seam (fig. 4–6).

**5.** Sew the pocket back and pillow top together, on three sides, in the ditch. This leaves a faced flap on all sides. Add buttons to correspond to the buttonholes.

**6.** Slip the pillow form into the pocket and fasten the buttons to complete your project.

## SHOW AND TELL PILLOW
## —Suzy Show

Full-sized patterns. Cut the templates on the line and add about ¼" allowances to the fabric pieces.

Full-sized patterns. Cut the templates on the line and add about ¼" allowances to the fabric pieces.

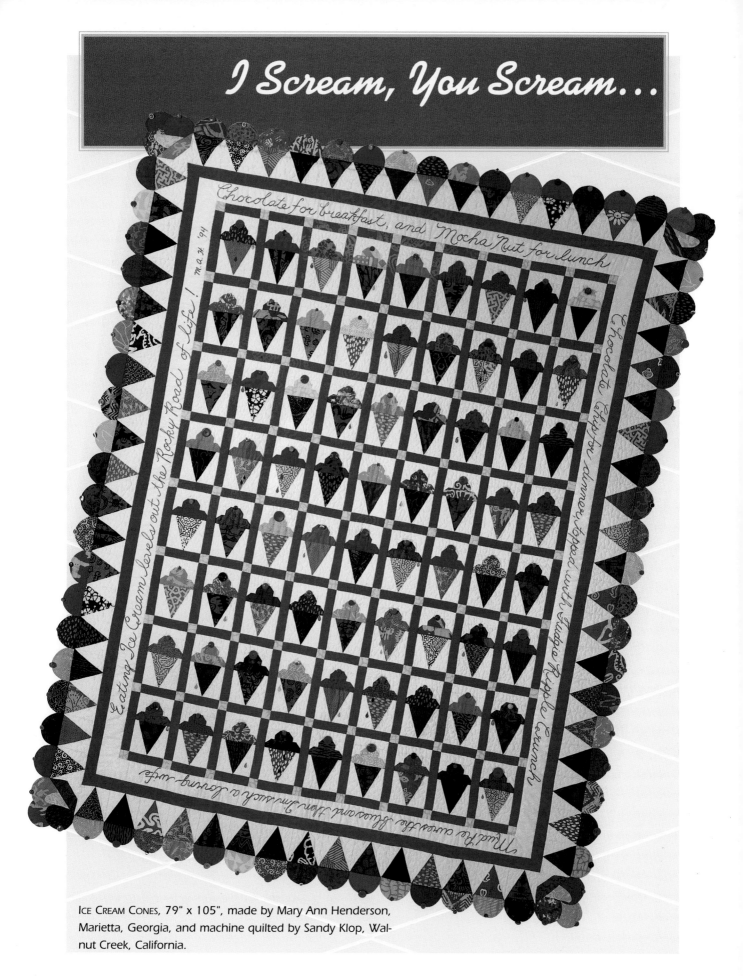

# I Scream, You Scream...

ICE CREAM CONES, 79" x 105", made by Mary Ann Henderson, Marietta, Georgia, and machine quilted by Sandy Klop, Walnut Creek, California.

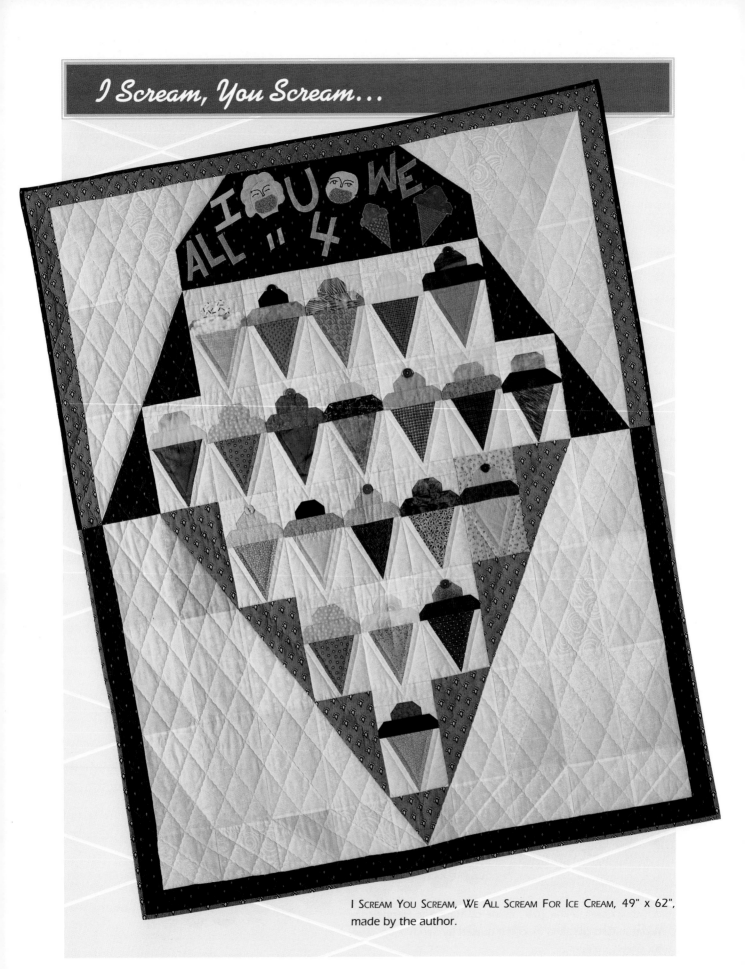

I SCREAM YOU SCREAM, WE ALL SCREAM FOR ICE CREAM, 49" x 62", made by the author.

Just who does not like a good ice cream cone? Just as appealing is the full-sized quilt (page 99) made by Mary Ann Henderson, Marietta, Georgia, and machine quilted by Sandy Klop, Walnut Creek, California. It sparkles with cherry button additions and a great saying, "Chocolate for breakfast, and Mocha Nut for lunch /Chocolate Chip for dinner, topped with Fudge Ripple Crunch/ Mud Pie cures the blues and then I'm such a loving wife/ Eating Ice Cream levels out the Rocky Road of life!"

**Quilt size: 49" x 62"**
**21 ice cream blocks: 5" x 9"**

## MATERIALS AND CUTTING

Refer to the chart on page 102.

## Quilt Assembly

**1.** Cut the 1⅝" background squares apart on the diagonal to make 84 half-square triangles for the F patches. Use the sew-and-flip method on page 104 to add the triangles to the B and C rectangles. It is optional whether you trim off the triangle underneath or leave it in place.

**2.** Referring to the block assembly diagram (fig. 4–7), piece the 21 ice cream cone blocks.

**3.** Piece the background rectangles (H and Hr), pairing light and medium-light fabrics.

**4.** Add the K triangles on each top corner of the M rectangle. Trim off the M fabric behind the K triangles, leaving a ¼" seam allowance.

**5.** Use a ruler and a pencil to hand draw "I SCREAM YOU SCREAM, WE ALL SCREAM FOR ICE CREAM," in your most folk fashion, onto freezer paper. Cut the freezer-paper templates on the drawn lines.

**6.** Press a lightweight fusible onto the wrong sides of your fabric pieces. Then press the freezer-paper templates onto the right sides. Cut the fabric pieces on the drawn lines.

**7.** Fuse the pieces in place on the M rectangle and add zigzag accents around faces and ice cream cones.

**8.** Complete the quilt by sewing the seven rows together. Notice that the bottom row is almost half size (fig. 4–8, page 103).

**9.** Add borders to the top and bottom. Complete the sides by piecing strips of different colors together.

**10.** The background is machine quilted with a serpentine stitch and a walking foot. Hand quilting accents the cone areas.

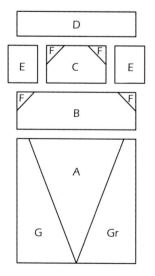

*Fig. 4–7.* Block assembly.

## MATERIALS AND CUTTING

| LOCATION | TOTAL YDS. | SCRAPS | CUT FROM EACH SCRAP | TO MAKE |
|---|---|---|---|---|
| **Ice cream cone blocks** | | | | |
| Cones | ⅔ | 21 pieces 6" x 6" | use template A | 21 A |
| Ice cream | ¾ | 21 pieces 5" x 7" | 1 rectangle 2" x 5½" | 21 B |
| | | | 1 rectangle 2" x 3" | 21 C |
| Background | 1½ | 21 pieces 7" x 11" | 1 rectangle 1½" x 5½" | 21 D |
| | | | 2 rectangles 1¾" x 2" | 42 E |
| | | | 4 squares 1⅝" x 1⅝" | 84 F |
| | | | use template G/Gr | 21 G and 21 Gr |
| **Quilt background** | | | | |
| Light | 1⅝ | 23 pieces 6" x 11" | use template H | 23 H |
| | | 4 pieces 6" x 7" | use template I | 8 I |
| | | 1 piece 4" x 6" | use template J | 1 J |
| | | 1 square 5½" x 5½" | cut diagonally once | 2 K |
| Medium light | 1⅝ | 23 pieces 6" x 11" | use template Hr | 23 Hr |
| | | 8 pieces 6" x 7" | use template Ir | 8 Ir |
| | | 1 piece 4" x 6" | use template Jr | 1 Jr |
| **Large ice cream cone** | | | | |
| Cone | ⅜ | 1 piece 11" x 24" | use template H/Hr | 3 H and 3 Hr |
| | | 1 piece 6" x 7" | use template L | 1 L |
| Topping | ⅜ | 1 piece 11" x 12" | use template H/Hr | 2 H and 2 Hr |
| | | 1 rectangle 9½" x 25½" | | 1 M |

| LOCATION | YARDS | CUTTING |
|---|---|---|
| Border | 1½ | strips 2½" wide |
| | | strips 2½" wide |
| Backing | 3¼ | 2 panels 34" x 53" (crosswise seam) |
| Batting | | 53" x 66" |
| Binding | ⅝ | 7 strips 2½" x 40" |

**Fig. 4–8.** Quilt assembly.

# Sew-and-Flip Triangles

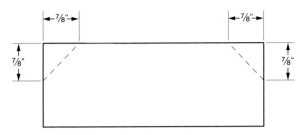

Fig. 4–9. Draw a line between the two marks.

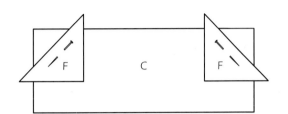

Fig. 4–10. Triangle placement for sewing.

To add the F triangles to the B and C rectangles, mark ⅞" from the corner, as shown (fig. 4–9). Draw a line between the two marks. This line represents the long edge of the F triangle.

Place the triangle, right sides together, with the long edge on the drawn line. Let the same amount of dog ear extend on each side (fig. 4–10).

Sew with a ¼" seam allowance, as measured from the edge of the triangle. Flip the triangle back and press. You can either leave the ice cream fabric underneath the triangle or snip it away, leaving a ¼" seam allowance.

## I Scream, You Scream...

### Full-sized patterns

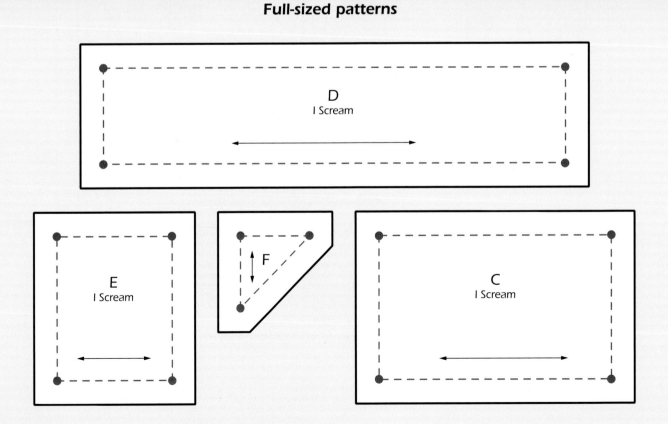

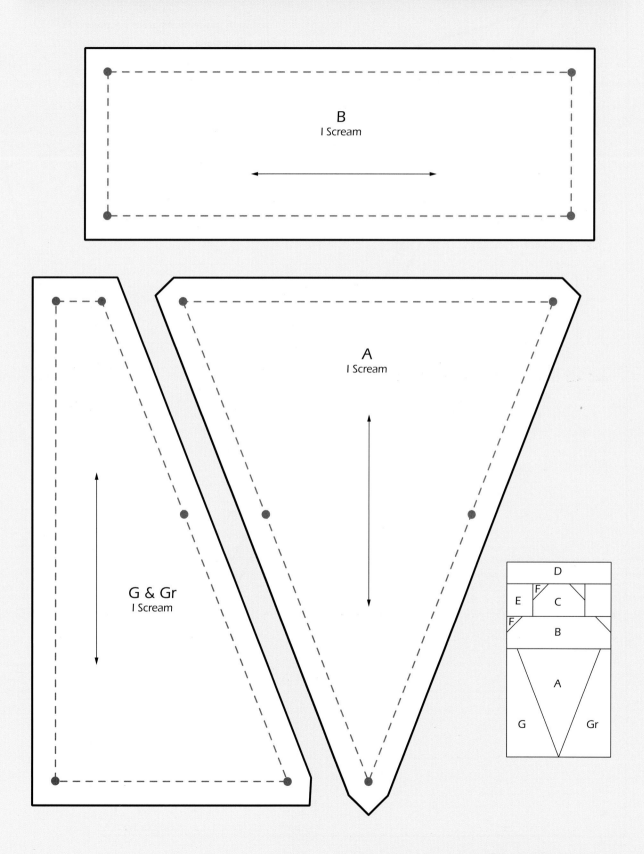

B
I Scream

A
I Scream

G & Gr
I Scream

D

F

E    C

F

B

A

G        Gr

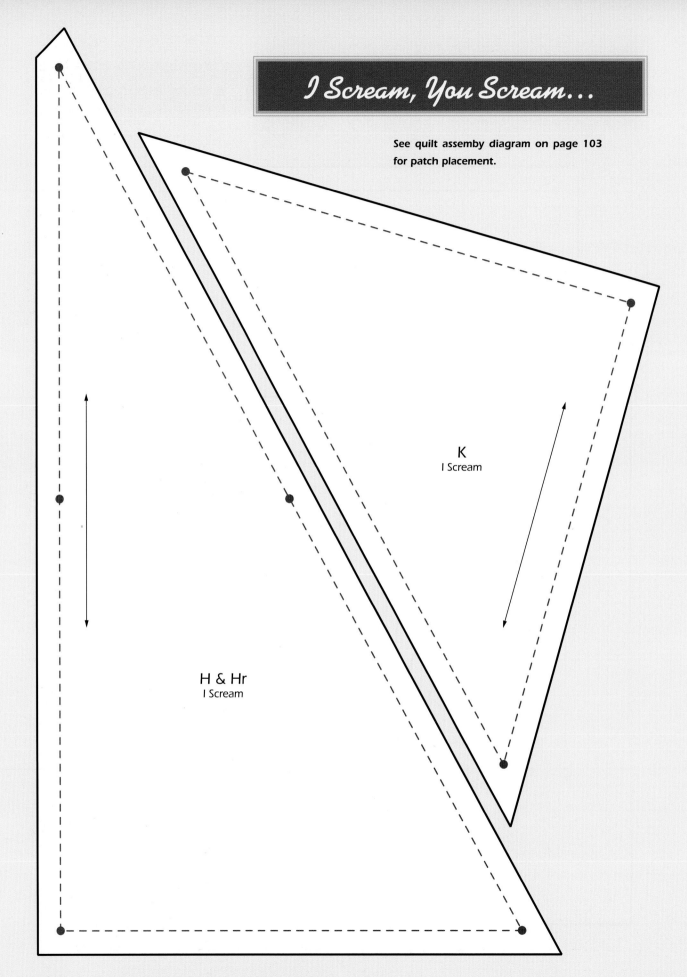

I Scream, You Scream...

See quilt assemby diagram on page 103 for patch placement.

K
I Scream

H & Hr
I Scream

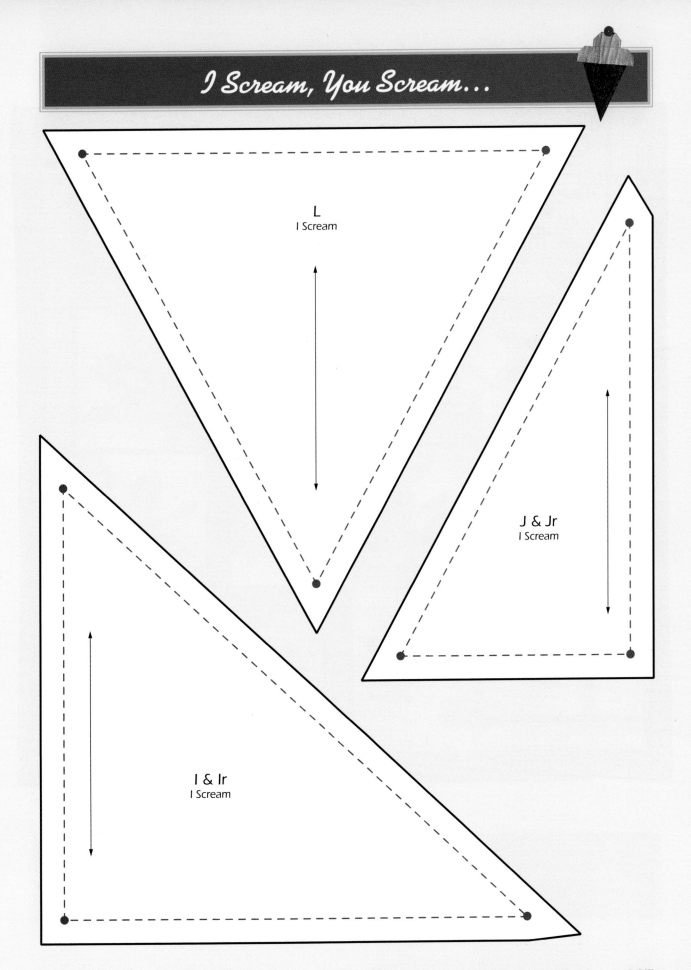

L
I Scream

J & Jr
I Scream

I & Ir
I Scream

PORTULACA, 51" x 51", by the author.

# Portulaca

# Portulaca

The classic basket pattern takes on a new dimension as it swirls around a field of brightly washed colors. It was easy to name this design Portulaca, once my flowers came into bloom.

**Quilt size: 51" x 51"**
**Finished block size: 10½"**

## MATERIALS AND CUTTING

| Location | Yards | First cut | Second cut | To make |
|---|---|---|---|---|
| **Background (can use scraps)** | | | | |
| pastels | 1½ | 16 squares 4" x 4" | | 16 C |
| | | 8 squares 6¼" x 6¼" | cut diagonally twice | 32 D |
| | | 32 rectangles 2½" x 7" | | 32 E |
| | | 8 squares 4⅞" x 4⅞" | cut diagonally once | 16 G |
| **Flowers (strip piece, see page 110)** | | | | |
| light | 1 (or mixed prints) | 16 strips 1¾" x 27" | | 128 B |
| dark | 1 (or mixed prints) | 16 strips 1¾" x 27" | | 128 B |
| Basket | ½ | 8 squares 5⅞" x 5⅞" | cut diagonally once | 16 A |
| | | 16 squares 2⅞" x 2⅞" | cut diagonally once | 32 F |
| Accent | ½ | 16 strips 1" x 11" | | 16 H |
| | | 4 squares 1" x 1" | | 4 I |
| inner border | | 8 strips 1" x 2½" | | 8 J |
| Inner border | ⅝ | 4 strips 2½" x 21½" | | |
| | | 4 strips 2½" x 23½" | | |
| Outer border | 1⅝ | 4 strips 2½" x 54" | | |
| Backing | 3¼ | 2 panels 28" x 55" | | |
| Batting | | 55" x 55" | | |
| Binding | ½ | 6 strips 2½" x 40 | | |

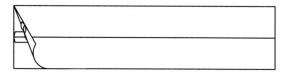

Fig. 4–11. Fold strip-set in half.

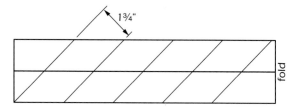

Fig. 4–12. Cut every 1¾", through both layers.

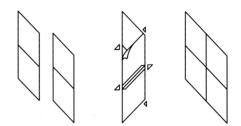

Fig. 4–13. Sew two diamond pairs to make a four-patch unit.

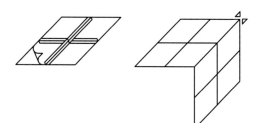

Fig. 4–14. Trim the dog ears.

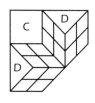

Fig. 4–15. Add the D and C patches.

## Quilt Assembly

### FLOWERS

**1.** For the strip-cut diamonds (B patches), stitch a light and a dark 1¾" x 27" strip together on a long side to make a strip-set. Press the seam allowances open. Fold the strip-set in half, wrong sides together (fig. 4–11).

**2.** Cut the folded strip-set at a 45-degree angle every 1¾" to make eight diamond pairs (fig. 4–12). Repeat these instructions for the remaining 1¾" x 20" strips, for a total of 128 diamond pairs.

**3.** Sew two diamond pairs together to form a four-patch unit. "Pin and peek" to check the center seam alignment. Press seam allowances open and trim the dog ears (fig. 4–13).

**4.** The D triangles and C squares are set into the diamonds with a Y-shaped seam. Join 2 four-patch units, by starting at the top edge and stopping ¼" from the bottom edge, where the three seams of the Y come together. End with a backstitch. Trim the dog ears (fig. 4–14). Sew 4 four-patches together for each basket.

**5.** Stitch the background D triangles to the diamonds. (For these Y seams, sew to the inside right angle, stop, and backstitch.) Trim the dog ears. Add the C squares in the same way (fig. 4–15).

**6.** For each block, add the A basket piece. Sew the F triangles to the background E rectangles, then attach these E–F units to the sides of the basket. End with corner triangle G (fig. 4–16).

**7.** Use a design wall or a flat surface to place the basket blocks in a pleasing, balanced arrangement. Stitch a narrow accent strip to the right of each basket (figure 4–17).

**8.** Sew the 1" square to a block, as shown in fig. 4–18. Be sure to stop at the ¼" seam line, leaving the seam allowances free.

**9.** Attach the remaining three blocks in a clockwise direction to complete one four-block section of the quilt (fig. 4–19). Make three more sections like this, then join the four sections, as shown in figure 4–20, page 112.

**9.** For the inner border, sew a 1" x 2½" accent piece (J) to one end of each inner border strip. Using one of each length, join the border strips together in sets of two. Then sew the inner borders to the quilt, matching the seams of the accent strips on the borders to the accent strips on the blocks. Complete the quilt with a dark outside border, with mitered corners.

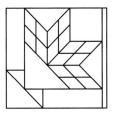

**Fig. 4–16.** Add the E, F, and G patches.

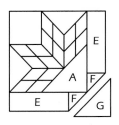

**Fig. 4–17.** Add an accent strip to the same side of each block.

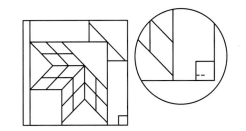

**Fig. 4–18.** Sew the center square, stopping at the seam line.

**Fig. 4–19.** Four-block section.

**Fig. 4–20.** Quilt assembly.

MY MILLENNIUM MEDALLION, 88" x 88", by the author.

Starting with a Dusty Miller block, this quilt radiates outward with additional rows, featuring Seminole patchwork, quick-piecing borders, appliqué inspired by stained glass, and ending with stair steps. The number of additional rows determines the size of the quilt. Stop when your heart and time desire. So I will always remember this turn-of-the-century quilt, I appliquéd "2001" right in the center.

**Quilt size: 88" x 88"**
**Dusty Miller block size: 16" x 16"**

## MATERIALS

Light background: 4 yards

Contrasting fabrics: 6 to 12 half-yard pieces

Binding: ¾ yard for straight-grain binding 2½" wide. Or use a 33" square for bias binding cut 2½" wide.

Backing: 8 yards

Batting: 92" x 92"

Iron-on grid paper

## Quilt Assembly

Refer to the quilt assembly diagram (fig. 4–22, page 115) while making your quilt.

### DUSTY MILLER BLOCK

**1.** Copy the D template (page 117) four times for paper piecing the rays. Starting at #1, sew and flip the remaining pieces in numerical order. Make four rays.

**2.** Stitch C to B four times. Sew the B/C units and the Ds together just up to the ¼" seam allowance. Remove the paper carefully.

Mark the ¼" seam allowance on all eight angles of A. Sew the B/C/D units to A, just up to the seam allowance and backstitch as before.

**3.** For the E patches, cut two squares 5⅝". Cut the triangles apart on one diagonal. Add the Es to the corners to complete the Dusty Miller block (fig. 4–21).

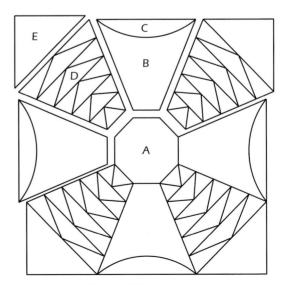

**Fig. 4–21.** Dusty Miller block assembly.

**Fig. 4–22.** Quilt assembly.

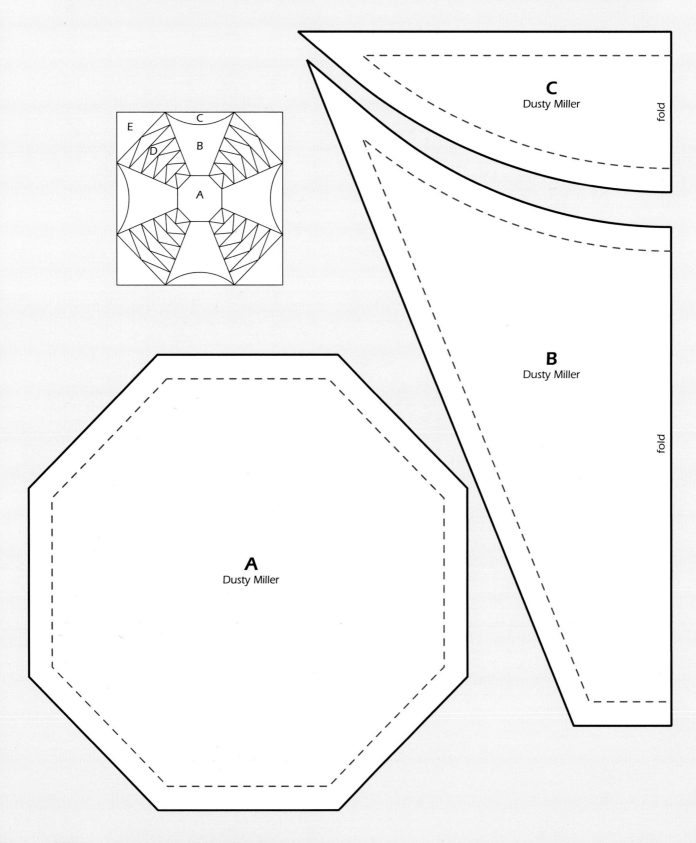

C
Dusty Miller

fold

B
Dusty Miller

fold

E
D
C
B
A

**A**
Dusty Miller

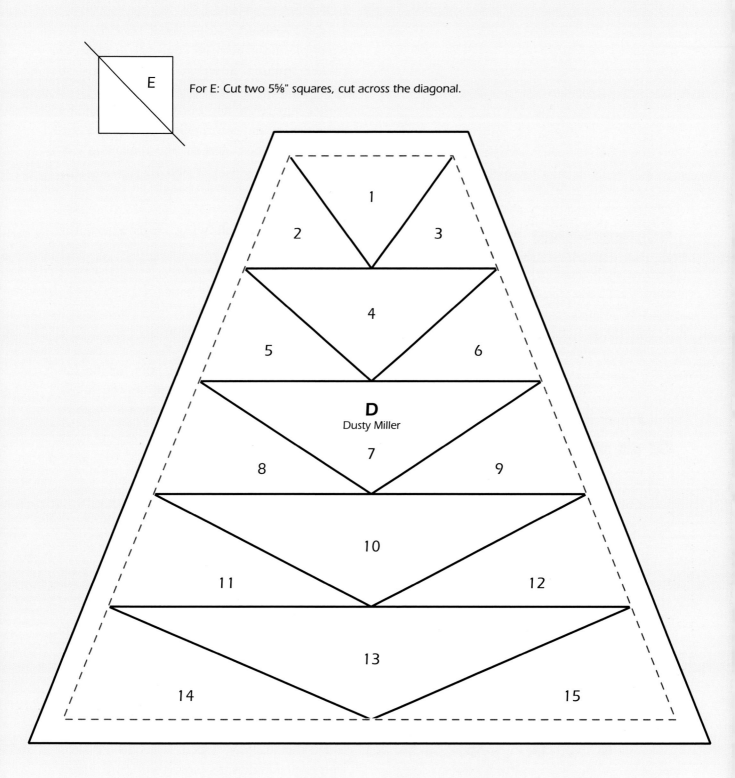

For E: Cut two 5⅝" squares, cut across the diagonal.

E

1

2

3

4

5

6

**D**
Dusty Miller

7

8

9

10

11

12

13

14

15

### BORDER 1, STRIPS

Cut four border strips 2½" x 16½". Use the paper-piecing pattern on page 121 to make 12 corner squares. Sew two border strips on opposite sides of the Dusty Miller block. Stitch corner squares to the ends of the remaining border strips and sew them to the top and bottom of the block. Reserve the remaining corner squares for borders 3 and 5.

### BORDER 2, SEMINOLE

**1.** Cut the following strips across the width of the fabrics:

    4 print strips 1¾" wide

    2 dark solid strips 1" wide

    2 print strips 1½" wide

    2 light solid strips 1" wide

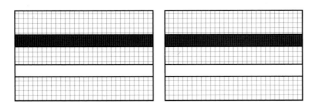

**Fig. 4–23.** Strip-sets.

**2.** Stitch five strips together, in the following order, to make each strip-set (fig. 4–23). Make two strip-sets. Press the seam allowances in the same direction.

    print strip 1¾"

    dark solid strip 1"

    print strip 1½"

    light solid strip 1"

    print strip 1¾"

**Fig. 4–24.** Cut the strip-sets into 1½" strips.

**3.** Cut the pieced strips into 1½" wide strips (fig. 4–24).

**4.** Cut one dark solid strip and one light solid strip 4½" wide across the fabrics. Cut again into strips 1" x 4½".

**5.** Sew the pieced and solid strips together, offsetting the dark and light colors to create the diagonal lattice. Note the ¾" drop with each addition. As pieced strips are added, align the previously sewn edges (fig. 4–25).

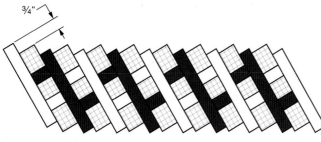

¾"

**Fig. 4–25.** Join the strips, alternating colors to create the lattice.

## Corners

*I resolved the corner addition through trial and error. The first attempt had a few mistakes that I actually concealed with a permanent magic marker. I could not live with that so off it came, to be replaced with a brighter, correct Seminole border.*

**1.** The secret? Make a freezer-paper template for the whole border that is 2" x 20" (inside) x 24" (outside). These are finished measurements.

**2.** Place the template on the right side of a Seminole border so that its ends balance, then press the template so it adheres to the border. Test the template on the other three borders before anything is cut.

**3.** Trim off the diagonal ends, leaving a ¼" seam allowance. You should have perfect mitered borders that match.

*Never press a freezer-paper template on the back side of a pieced block because the raw edges of the seam allowance will fray when pulled free.*

## BORDER 3, STRIPS

Cut four border strips 2½" x 24½". Sew two border strips on opposite sides of the quilt. Stitch corner squares, made during border 1 construction, to the ends of the remaining border strips and sew them to the top and bottom.

## BORDER 4
## HALF-SQUARE TRIANGLE UNITS

**1.** Cut 14 sets of contrasting squares 4⅞". Quick piece these to yield 28 half-square triangle units.

**2.** Make four corner squares (pattern on page 121).

**3.** Take time to place the units in a pleasing arrangement. A design wall helps here. Stitch seven half-square triangle units together for each border strip.

**4.** Sew two strips on opposite sides of the quilt. Sew the four corner blocks to the ends of the remaining strips and stitch in place.

## BORDER 5, STRIPS

Cut four strips 2½" x 32½". Repeat the border 3 instructions, including corner squares.

## BORDER 6, APPLIQUÉ

**1.** Cut 20 background squares 8½", for the appliqué.

**2.** Make iron-on grid templates for pieces 1–4 from the pattern on page 124.

**3.** Press the templates onto the right sides of your chosen fabrics, aligning the fabric grain line with the template grid. Cut out the fabric pieces on the line.

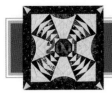

**4.** Appliqué the pieces to the background in numerical order, as follows: Pin the piece in place on the background and straight stitch next to the paper edges. Trim off excess fabric up to the paper edge.

**5.** Remove the paper and place a lightweight stabilizer underneath and machine satin stitch to cover the raw edges.

**6.** Sew four sets of five blocks together for the border strips. Sew two strips on opposite sides of the quilt.

**7.** Make four corner squares from the 8" paper-piecing pattern on pages 122–123. Stitch these to the ends of the remaining borders and sew the adjacent sides.

## BORDER 7, FOUR-PATCHES

Cut 224 squares 2½". Mixing the fabrics, make 56 Four-Patch blocks from the squares.

## BORDER 8, STRIPS

Cut two strips 2½" x 64½" and two strips 2½" x 68½". Sew the 64½" strips to the top and bottom of the quilt, then the 68½" strips to the sides.

## BORDER 9, STAIR STEPS

Make 36 blocks (includes the four corners). The finished blocks measure 8" square.

*I made each block individually so that each has a color variation.*

**These directions are for one block:**

**1.** Select a light and a dark fabric for the half-square triangles in the stair steps. Use quick-piecing to make seven half-square triangle units, cut 2⅞" square.

**2.** For the background, cut from medium fabric two squares 2½", two rectangles 2½" x 4½", and one rectangle 2½" x 6½".

**3.** Arrange the half-square triangle units to create the risers and the tops of the steps. Fill in the block with the background squares and rectangles. Stitch in vertical strips, then sew the strips together (fig. 4–26).

**4.** Note the connector unit in the middle of each border: Cut eight rectangles in mixed

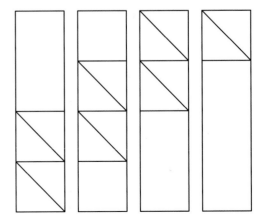

**Fig. 4–26.** Stair Steps block assembly.

colors 2½" x 4½". Make 16 half-square triangle units by quick piecing eight light and eight dark 2⅞" squares. Arrange and sew the pieces into four connector units.

**5.** For each border strip, arrange the eight Stair Steps blocks with a connector unit in the middle. Sew the blocks and units together to make four border strips.

**6.** Sew a border strip to opposite sides of the quilt. Add Stair Steps blocks to each end of the remaining border strips and sew these to the top and bottom of the quilt.

## BORDER 10, STRIPS

Cut four strips 2½" x 90". Sew the strips to the quilt and miter the corners.

## FINISHING

Layer the backing, batting, and quilt top. Baste and quilt the layers and bind the raw edges.

*I basted and quilted with wool batting which was like going through butter, using variegated thread. The changing colors make the quilting interesting. A supported lap hoop aided in the lap quilting process. Binding completes the quilt.*

## Border 1 and Border 4 corners

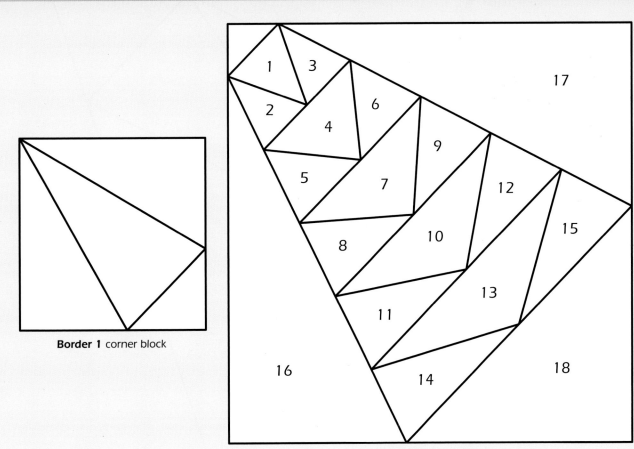

**Border 1** corner block

**Border 4** corner block

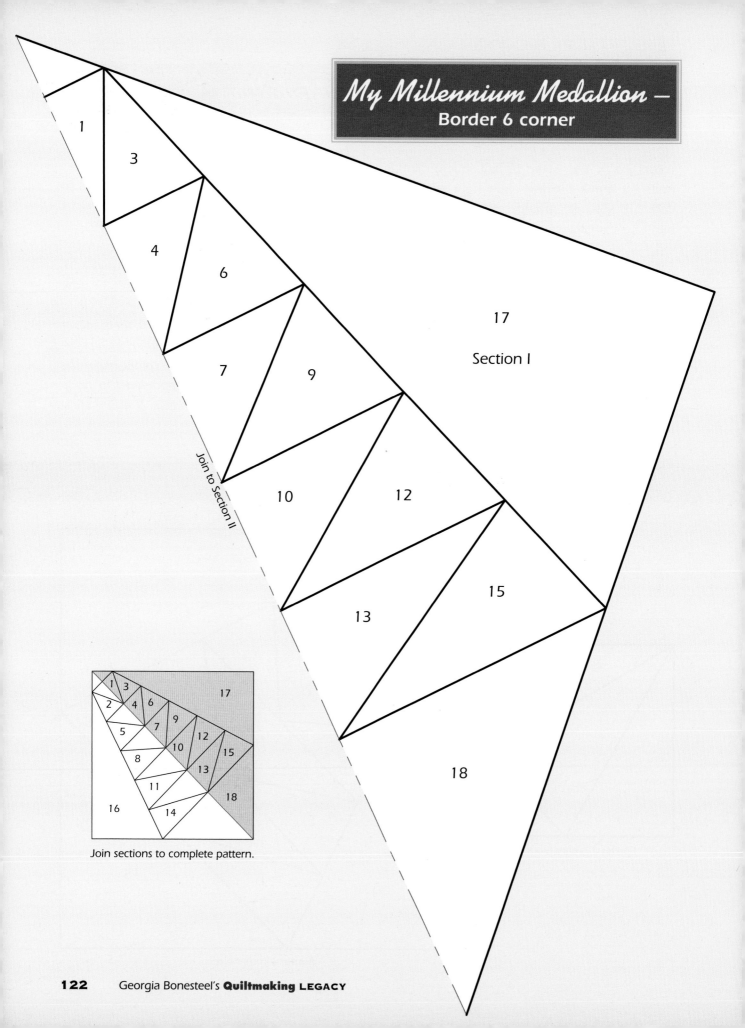

My Millennium Medallion —
Border 6 corner

1

3

4

6

7

9

17

Section I

Join to Section II

10

12

13

15

18

Join sections to complete pattern.

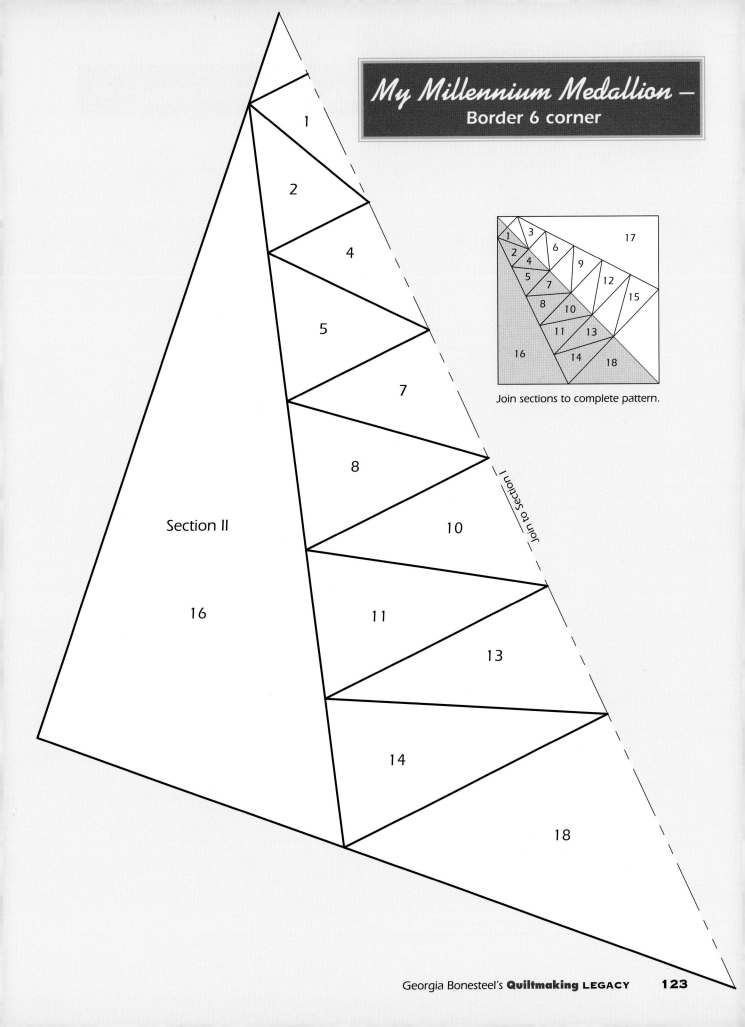

My Millennium Medallion —
Border 6 corner

1
2
4
5
7
8
10
11
13
14
18
16
Section II

Join to Section I

1
3
17
2
6
4
9
5
7
12
8
15
11
13
16
14
18

Join sections to complete pattern.

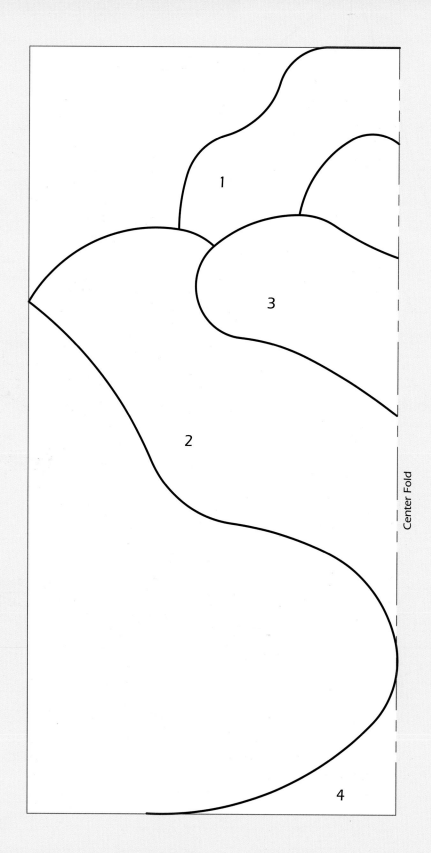

1

3

2

Center Fold

4

# Posies 'Round The Pickle Dish

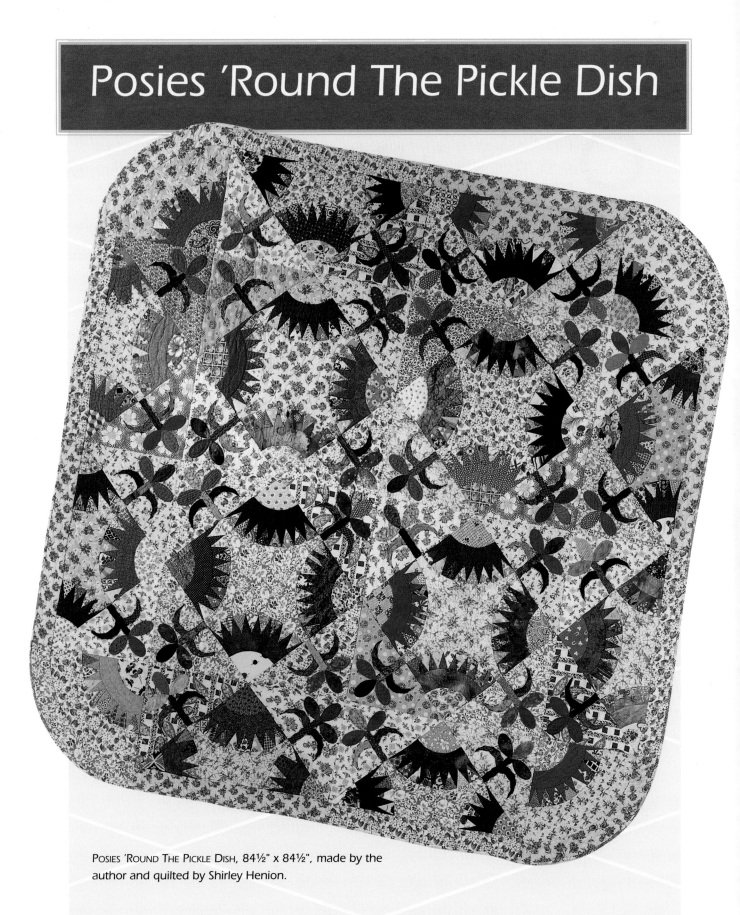

POSIES 'ROUND THE PICKLE DISH, 84½" x 84½", made by the
author and quilted by Shirley Henion.

# Posies 'Round The Pickle Dish

Of all the aspects of quiltmaking, the one that amazes me the most is feed sacks. Their supply is never ending. Their uniqueness is intriguing. They prompt stories from the past and rekindle history. Teaching this quilt at my Freedom Escape quilt retreat resulted in a panorama of colors and sizes and some very good pickle recipes.

**Quilt size, 90¾" x 90¾"**
**Block size, 20" x 20"**

## MATERIALS

| Location | Yards | First Cut | Second Cut | To Make |
|---|---|---|---|---|
| **Pickle Dish** | | | | |
| | 2¼ | Templates | | 4 A and 8 half A |
| | 1 | Templates | | 28 B and16 half B |
| | 1 | Templates | | 28 C and 16 half C |
| | 1¼ | Paper piecing | | D and half D (arcs) |
| | 1⅓ | Paper piecing | | E (arcs) |
| **Posies** | | | | |
| Background | 3⅝ | 16 squares 15" x 15" | cut diagonally once | 32 F |
| Stem | ¼ | Template | | 32 G |
| Leaf | ½ | Template | | 32 H and 32 Hr |
| Flower petal | 1¼ | Template | | 96 I |
| **Finishing** | | | | |
| Corners | 1 | Template | | 4 J |
| Border | 1⅜ | Template | | 4 K |
| | | 8 strips 3½" x 20½" | | 8 L |
| Backing | 8⅜ | 3 panels 32" x 95" | | |
| Batting | | 95" x 95" | | |
| Binding | 1 | 1 square 32" x 32" | 2½" wide bias strips | |

## Quilt Assembly

**1.** For paper piecing, trace the D/E arc pattern 28 times onto lightweight paper. Make 16 copies of the half arc pattern also. Be sure to add a ¼" seam allowance to the border side of all half templates.

**2.** Starting at the center D template, sew and flip the E and D pieces to complete all the paper-pieced arcs and half arcs. Trim the sewn arcs, leaving ¼" seam allowances beyond the paper pattern on all sides. Remove the paper templates.

**3.** Sew the B and C patches to the pieced arcs. Then sew the B/C arc units to the A patches by aligning the midpoint of A with the center D point on the arcs. Make four whole Pickle Dish blocks (finish 20") and eight half blocks (figure 4–27).

**4.** Sew the J patches to the remaining B/C/arc units to complete the corner blocks.

*To sew a curved seam, align the centers of the pieces and pin the ends. Sew with the pieced arcs against the feed dogs.*

**5.** Use your favorite stitch to appliqué the stems, leaves, and petals to the F triangles.

*The raw edges of the stems and leaves in my quilt (photo on page 125) were sewn with a satin stitch in variegated thread. The edges of the petals were turned by spraying them with sizing and pressing them over a manila folder template. A small running stitch with matching thread was used to secure the petals on the very edge.*

**6.** Sew the appliquéd F triangles to the Pickle Dish blocks and half blocks. Referring to the quilt assembly diagram (fig. 4–28), sew the blocks together in rows, then sew the rows together.

**7.** Add a 3" border around the outside using curved template K for the corners.

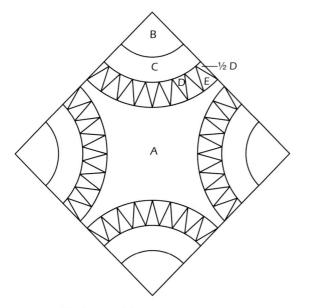

**Fig. 4–27.** Block assembly.

**Pimento and Cucumber Pickles**

*(Martha Adsit)*

4 qts. cut cucumber (pared)

1 qt. onions

1 cup pimentos (canned are best)

1 T whole mustard

1 tsp. celery seed

3 cups white sugar

1 T. salt

1 qt. vinegar

Leave the cucumbers whole or cut very fine. Put all in a kettle, mix, and let boil for 6 to 8 minutes. Can immediately.

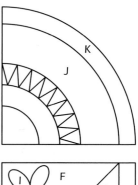

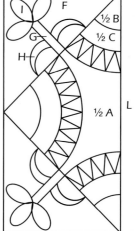

**Fig. 4–28.** Quilt assembly.

## Eugenia's Garlic Pickles

*(made best by my mother, Virginia W. Jinkinson)*

> 1 large bottle of sour pickles (The hardest part of this recipe is finding the sour pickles.)
>
> 4½ lbs. sugar
>
> 8 cloves garlic, peeled
>
> 2 T. pickling spices in cheesecloth

Dump the pickles into the sink and wash out the jar. Cut the stems and butt ends off the pickles. Cut them into ½" slices and place in a colander with ice cubes on top, overnight. In the washed jar, layer the pickles with sugar. Add a clove of garlic and the pickling spices. Let the pickles age in the refrigerator for a couple of days. Turn the jar upside down frequently as the juices form.

## Joanie's Pickles

*(Joan McMullen)*

> 7 lbs. cucumbers
>
> 2 gal. water
>
> 3 cups hydrated lime (pickling lime)
>
> 6 cups apple cider vinegar
>
> 5 lbs. sugar
>
> 1 T. whole cloves
>
> ½ tsp. celery seed

Soak sliced cukes in limewater 24 hours. Drain and rinse. Soak in water for four hours, changing the water every hour. Drain well and put the cucumbers in a large pot with the other four ingredients. Bring it to a boil and pour over the cukes. Let stand overnight, then bring to a slow boil. Simmer 45 minutes and pack into hot, sterile jars. (Makes 10–11 pints.)

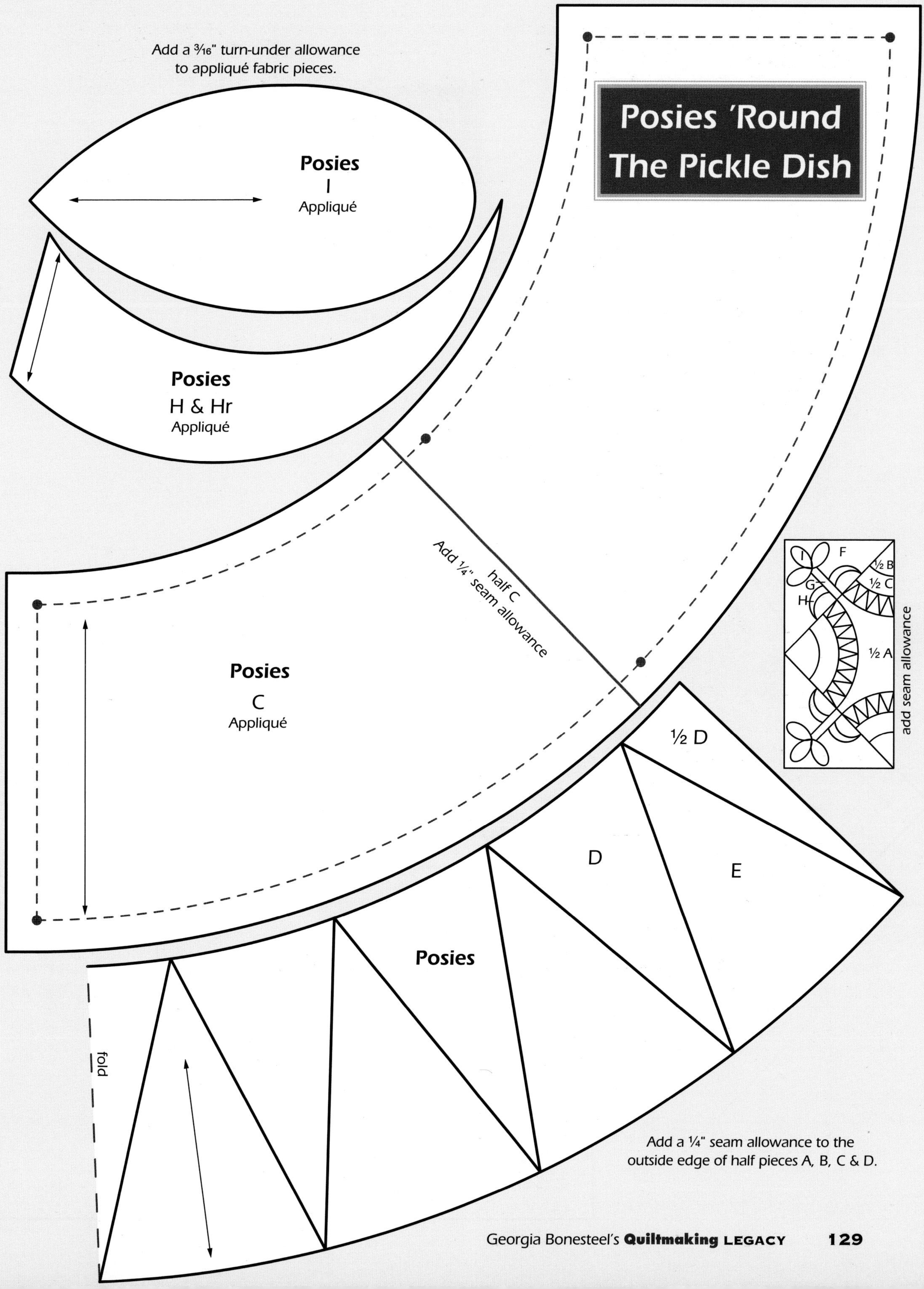

Add a ³⁄₁₆" turn-under allowance
to appliqué fabric pieces.

**Posies**
I
Appliqué

**Posies**
H & Hr
Appliqué

**Posies 'Round
The Pickle Dish**

Add ¼" seam allowance

half C

**Posies**
C
Appliqué

½ D

D

E

½ B
½ C
½ A

add seam allowance

**Posies**

fold

Add a ¼" seam allowance to the
outside edge of half pieces A, B, C & D.

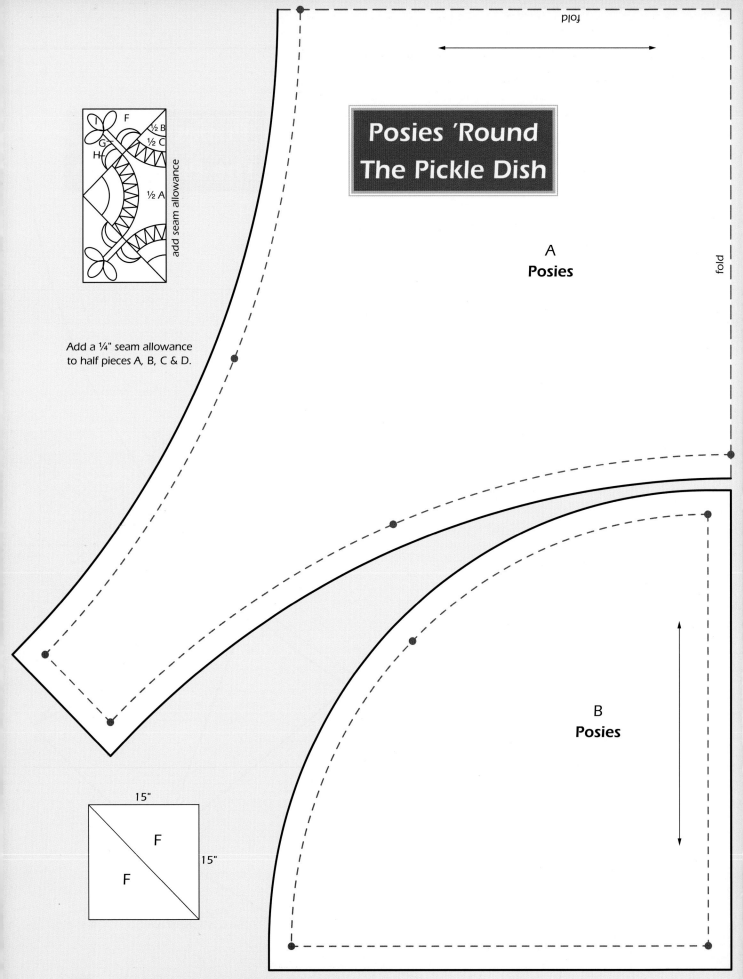

add seam allowance

½ B
½ C

½ A

F
G→
H

Add a ¼" seam allowance
to half pieces A, B, C & D.

Posies 'Round
The Pickle Dish

A
**Posies**

fold

fold

fold

B
**Posies**

15"

F

15"

F

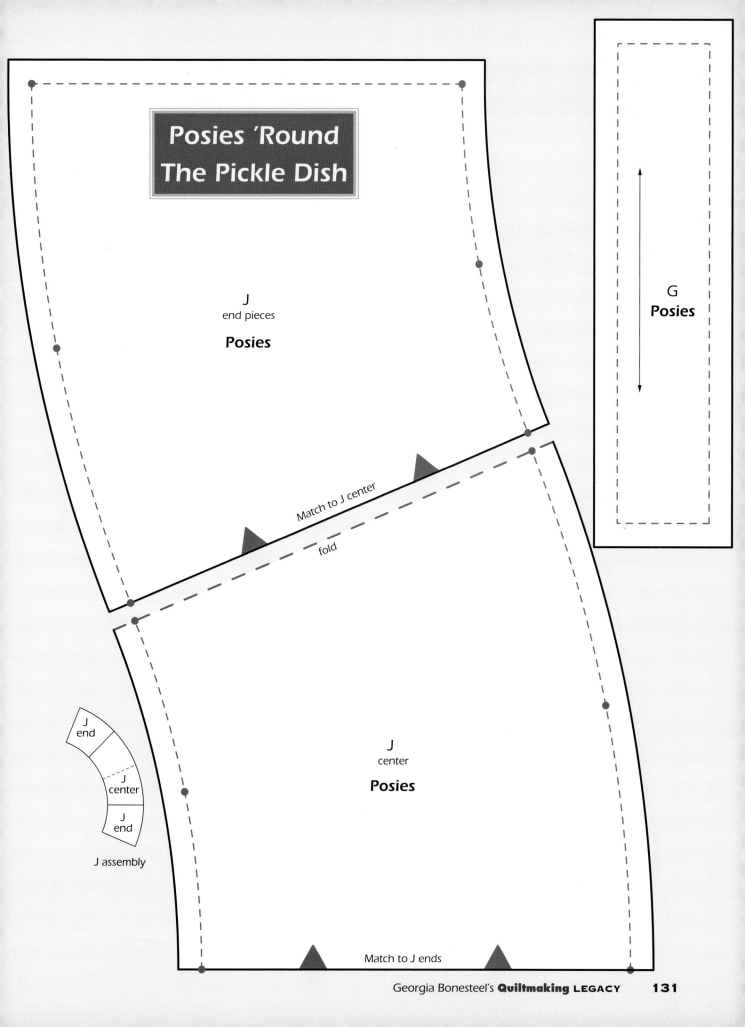

# Posies 'Round The Pickle Dish

J
end pieces

**Posies**

Match to J center

fold

J
center

**Posies**

G
**Posies**

J
end

J
center

J
end

J assembly

Match to J ends

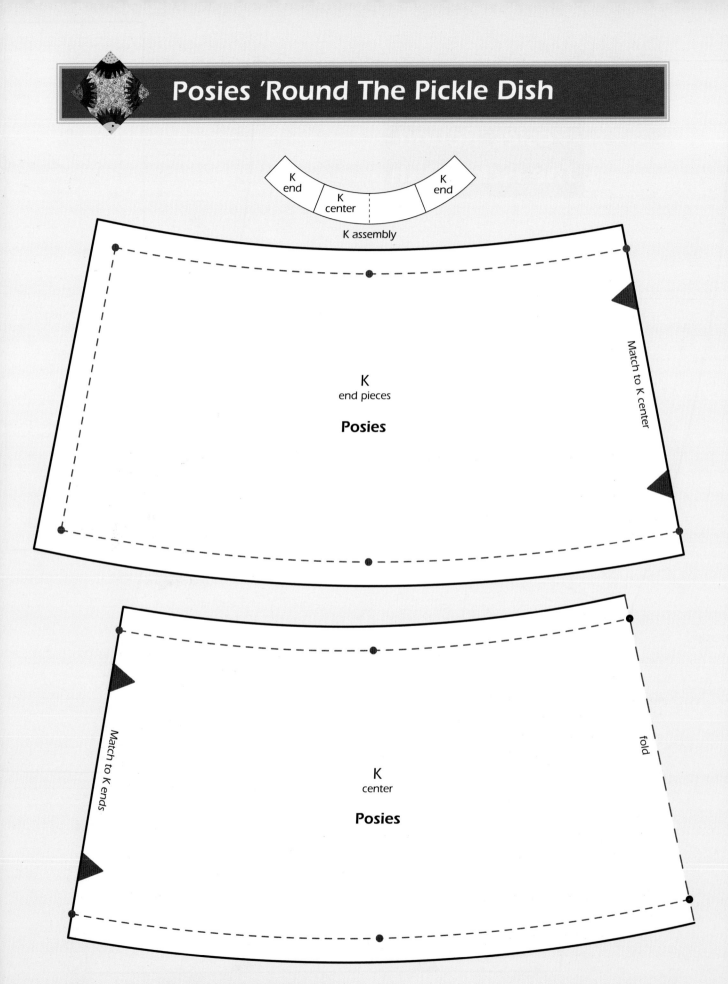

K
end

K
center

K
end

K assembly

K
end pieces

**Posies**

Match to K center

K
center

**Posies**

Match to K ends

fold

# Chapter 5

# *Just Got to Make*

As a quilter, I want to try it all and tackle the unusual. Sometimes I just fall into these novelty ideas through my television experiences, and others just pop into my head.

A lifetime's worth of tote bags have finally found a home. You can just tote so much stuff, so why not put the totes to better use in a quilt. Another taping trip exposed me to photo transfer, and now we can capture our memories on fabric. I was amazed at the Japanese Fishermen's Coats, and just had to try my hand at the persimmon stitch. The combination of white stitching on a navy blue background is so sharp and clear.

You can imagine television taping in a foreign country. It takes planning, organization, phone calls, e-mails, and many reservations. Then, once we arrive, there are the new roads, language changes, and different ways of living. The television equipment is cumbersome, but necessary.

One spring, when we arrived in Lenk, Switzerland, in a snowstorm, we were a bit perplexed to discover our quilt lesson was to be a "Chick on a Stick!" (See the Happy Chicken pattern, page 141). I had no idea chickens could be so popular. They are not only fun to make, but they have perked my interest in real chickens. Have fun making yours!

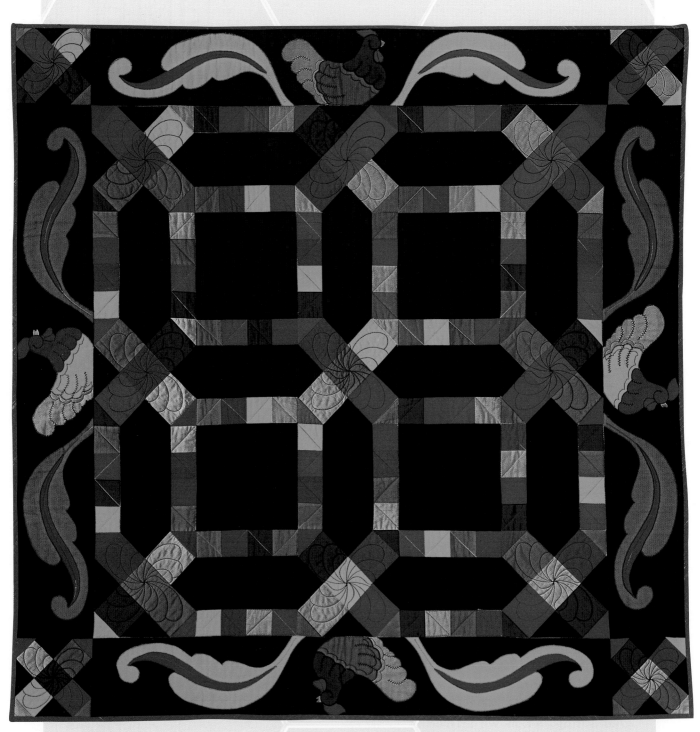

GARDEN MAZE WALL HANGING, 52" x 52", by the author.

# Garden Maze Wall Hanging

# Garden Maze Wall Hanging

Two connecting blocks form an interlaced design with an Amish style. Choose a medley of bright fabrics to set against a contrasting background. The chicken and swag border was inspired by my kitchen wallpaper.

**Quilt size, 52" x 52"**
**Block size, 8" x 8"**

## MATERIALS AND CUTTING

| Fabric | Yards | First cut | | Second cut | To make |
|---|---|---|---|---|---|
| Background | 1⅞ | | | | |
| | | 4 squares | 8½" x 8½" | | 4 A |
| | | 12 rectangles | 4½" x 8½" | | 12 C |
| | | 9 squares | 5¼" x 5¼" | cut diagonally twice | 36 E |
| (border) | | 4 strips | 6½" x 40½" | | 4 G |
| | | 4 squares | 4¼" x 4¼" | cut diagonally twice | 16 I |
| Brights (8 assorted, each 9" x 40", includes appliqué pieces) | | | | | |
| | | 96 squares | 2½" x 2½" | | 96 B |
| | | 45 squares | 3⅜" x 3⅜" | | 45 D |
| | | 18 squares | 2⅞" x 2⅞" | cut diagonally once | 36 F |
| | | 20 squares | 2⅝" x 2⅝" | | 20 H |
| | | 8 squares | 2⅜" x 2⅜" | cut diagonally once | 16 J |
| Backing | 3¼ | 2 panels | 28½" x 56" | | |
| Batting | | 56" x 56" | | | |
| Binding | ½ | 6 strips | 2½" x 40" | | |

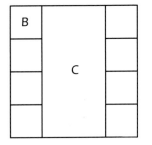

**Fig. 5–1.** Block 1.

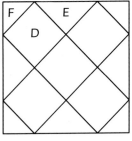

Block 2.

## Quilt Assembly

**1.** Make iron-on grid templates from the chicken and feather patterns (pages 138–139). Cut the chickens and feathers from bright fabrics.

*Press the grid-paper templates on fabric that has been pressed with sizing for stability. I used a reverse buttonhole stitch to attach the appliqué pieces.*

**2.** Referring to figure 5–1, make twelve of block 1, nine of block 2, and four corner blocks. Figure 5–2 shows how to press the allowances for block 2 and the corner block. Twirl the seam allowances at the intersections after releasing ¼" of the allowances.

**3.** Balancing the colors, lay out blocks 1 and 2 and the A squares into five rows, as shown in the quilt assembly diagram (fig. 5–3). Sew the blocks together in rows, then sew the rows together (fig. 5–4).

**5.** Use a reverse buttonhole stitch to appliqué a chicken design onto the center of each border strip. Continue with the feathers.

**6.** Sew a corner block to each end of two border strips. Stitch the other two border strips to the quilt. Finish with the border/corner block strips.

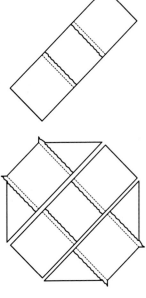
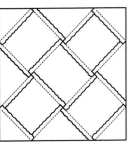

**Fig. 5–2.** Seam allowance pressing for block 2 and the corner block.

*Rather than hand quilt a feather design with black thread on black fabric, I used my embroidery module for perfect feathers and a twirl each time. (Didn't your mother ever tell you never to knit with black yarn!) For the other areas, I used my walking foot, variegated thread, and a narrow zigzag. Remember that a straight line is not forgiving, but a slight angle is more forgiving.*

**Fig. 5–3.** Quilt assembly.

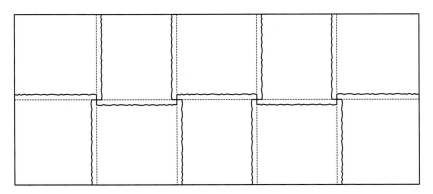

**Fig. 5–4.** Sew the blocks together in rows. Note the twirl at the seam intersections.

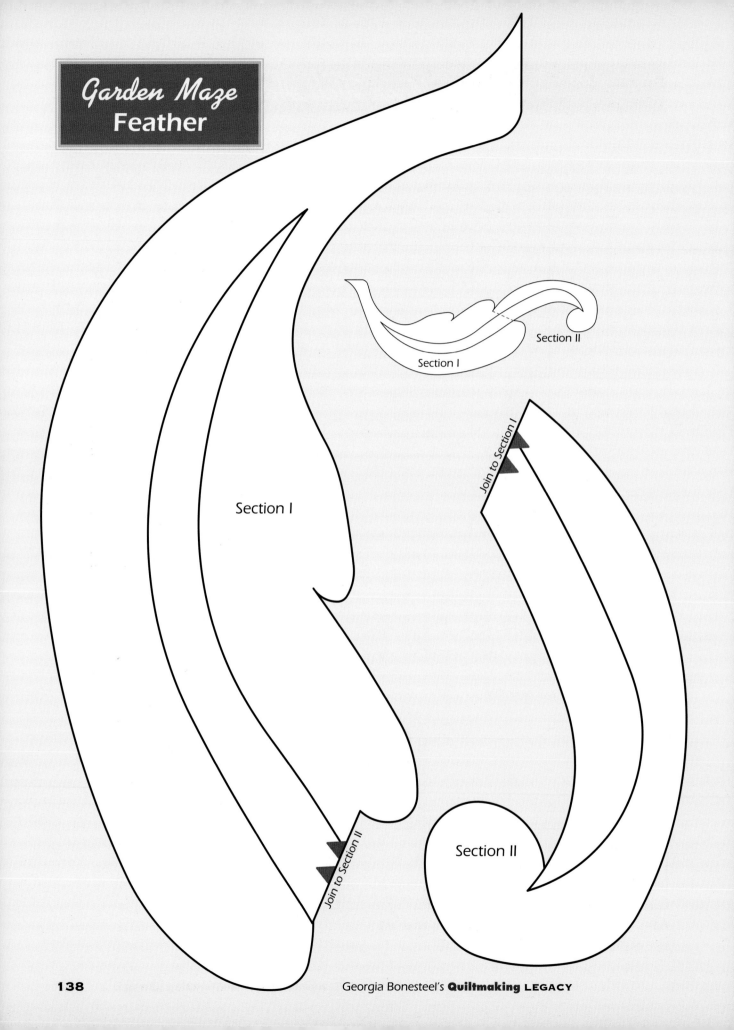

Garden Maze
Feather

Section I

Section II

Section I

Section II

Join to Section I

Join to Section II

# Happy Chicken or Chick on a Stick

Whatever you call this plump bird, it is fun and very appealing. It is what we learned in Lenk, Switzerland, for one of my television shows, years ago. It comes from a Danish design via the Swiss quilt shop Patch Art, and was altered over the years for a more American version.

**Size, about 9" x 9"**

## MATERIALS AND CUTTING

Cut 3 squares 9½". Cut the squares on one diagonal to make 6 triangles (2 for the wings and 4 for the body).

Cut 1 square 9½" for the base of the body

Cut 1 yellow hexagon (pattern on page 145) for the beak and 4 red hexagons for the comb and wattle.

Stuffing: cedar chips, polyester, plastic popcorn or dog ears from years of patchwork!

Small pieces of batting for wings, legs, and wattle

Two yellow fabrics cut 7" x 18" for legs

Two buttons for eyes

## Assembly

**1.** Make the beak and comb by folding the hexagons as shown in figure 5–5. Note how the comb pieces interlock.

**2.** Make the wattle by placing a running stitch around the edges of the hexagon and gathering it with a small amount of batting inside (figure 5–6, page 142).

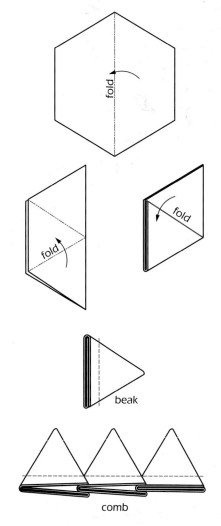

**Fig. 5–5.** Hexagon folds for beak and comb pieces.

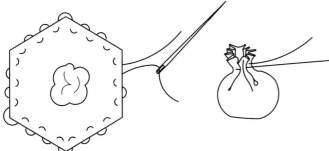

**Fig. 5–6.** Wattle construction.

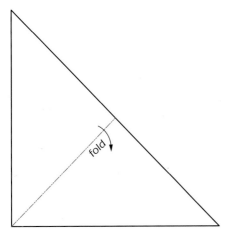

**Fig. 5–7.** Fold the wing triangle in half.

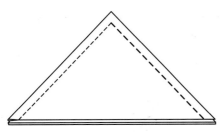

**Fig. 5–8.** Stitch along the short sides.

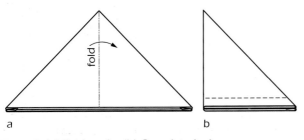

a           b

**Fig. 5–9.** (a) Fold again. (b) Completed wing.

**3.** For each wing, fold the triangle in half, right sides together (fig. 5–7). Cut a thin batting piece the same size as the folded triangle.

**4.** With the batting underneath and against the feed dogs, stitch on each short side of the triangle (fig. 5–8).

**5.** Turn the wing right side out and fold again. Baste along the raw edge (fig. 5–9).

**6.** Pin the wing on the short side of a body triangle (right side up), about 4¼" down from the top. Make certain that the folded part of the wing will be on top when the bird is assembled. Place another body triangle on top, right sides together, and stitch, catching the wing in the seam allowance (fig. 5–10). Repeat for the second wing to complete the two wing units.

**7.** Pin or baste the beak toward the top of one wing unit. Below that, place the wattle. Pin or baste the comb on the other side of the wing unit, as shown (fig. 5–11).

**8.** Place the second wing unit on top, right sides together, and sew along the two short sides, leaving the long side open. Turn the chicken right side out to see how it looks so far (fig. 5–12).

**9.** To make the legs, place the two yellow rectangles, right sides together. Draw around the legs, adding 12" for the leg length.

**10.** Place a thin rectangle of batting underneath the yellow rectangles. With the batting against the feed dogs, stitch around each leg on the drawn line.

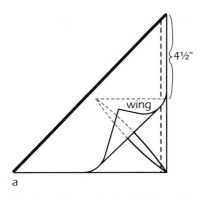

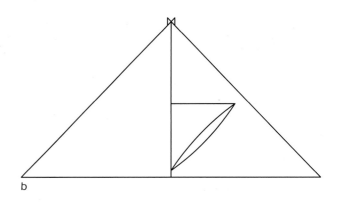

**Fig. 5–10.** Sewing wing to body: (a) Sew wing between two body triangles. (b) Completed wing unit.

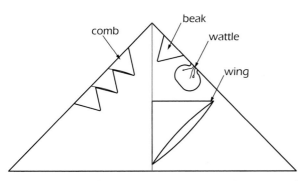

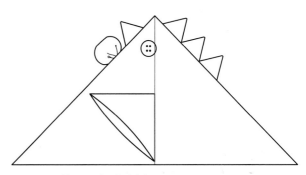

**Fig. 5–11.** Place the beak, wattle, and comb on one of the wing units.

**Fig. 5–12.** Top unit of chicken.

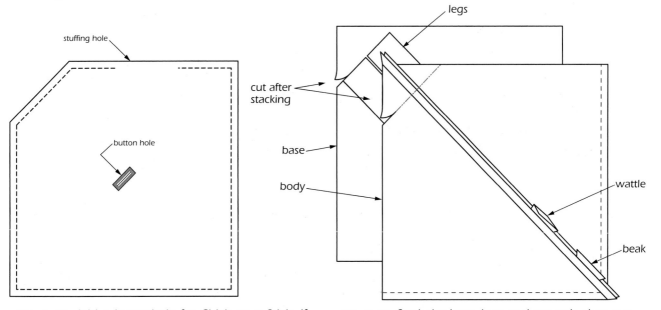

**Fig. 5–13.** Add a buttonhole for Chick on a Stick, if desired.

**Fig. 5–14.** Stack the base, legs, and top unit, then cut the corner along the edges of the legs.

**11.** Cut out each leg with a narrow (approx. ⅛") seam allowance and closer around the toes. Turn the legs right side out and press lightly. Form a gentle knot for the knee area.

**12.** If you want your Chick on a Stick, place a reinforced buttonhole in the center of the base fabric square (fig. 5–13, page 143). Pin the legs in position at one corner of the base of the body.

**13.** With the top unit turned inside out again, position it on the legs (fig. 5–14, page 143). After stacking the pieces, cut the corner off of the base and the top unit, following the top edge of the legs, as shown.

**14.** Pin the base to the top unit and sew around the edge, with a ¼" seam allowance, catching the legs in the seam and leaving a small side opening. Turn the chicken right side out through the opening, sew on the eyes, and fill with your favorite stuffing. Whipstitch the opening closed.

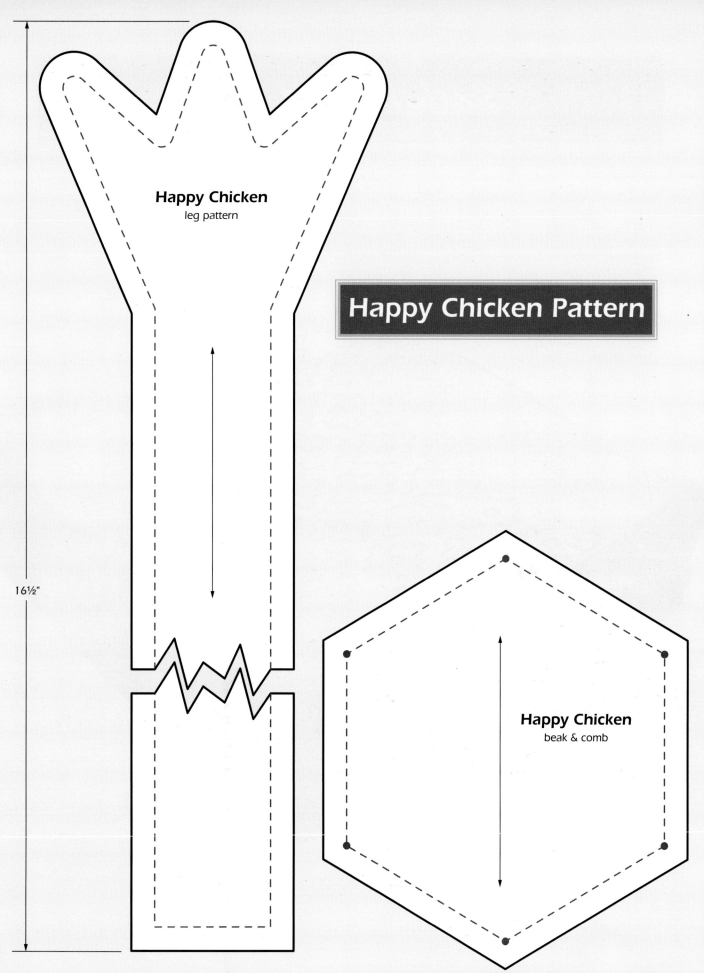

**Happy Chicken**
leg pattern

16½"

**Happy Chicken Pattern**

**Happy Chicken**
beak & comb

# Sashiko Soft Box

It was after viewing an exhibit of Japanese Fishermen's Coats from the Awaji Islands that I truly appreciated the simplicity of the quilted stitch on three layers of fabric. I experimented with the bib on a shirt and a kimono for my grandchild, Ellery. Choose a loosely woven fabric for ease in stitching by testing with a needle. A tight weave makes it difficult to stitch. Fabric with a woven stripe or plaid aids in following the lines.

This square, soft box can be used for thread storage or a napkin holder. The lid welcomes sashiko stitching, highlighted with the persimmon design. The soft box is made in two separate sections. First, the lid is made with sashiko hand stitching. Then the base and sides are assembled so the finished lid can be inserted to one open side. Quilting completes the box before the sides are whipstitched together.

**Finished Size: 9" square x 3" deep**

## MATERIALS AND CUTTING

Box base fabric: 9½"x 9½"

Box sides: one light and one dark strip, each 3⅞" x 23¼"

Lid: box fabric and two linings 9¾" x 9¾". The second lining piece will be used as the middle layer in place of batting.

Box lining: 16" x 16"

Box batting: 16" x 16"

Button loop: 1" x 6" box fabric bias strip

Decorative button

## Box Assembly

**1.** To make the button tab, fold the 1" x 6" bias strip in half lengthwise, right sides together. Sew along its length with a ¼" seam allowance, then turn the tube right side out.

**2.** Center and pin the button loop (sized to fit the button) on the front of the box lid fabric square, on the right side of the fabric, with raw edges aligned.

Kimono for Ellery. The latest grandchild sports a kimono with three layers of indigo blue fabric. Sashiko hand stitching highlights the sleeves, yoke, and midriff.

PHOTO: FROM THE AUTHOR.

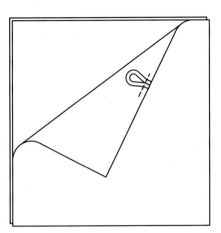

Fig. 5–15. Stack pieces in this order: one lining either side up, one lining right side up, box lid wrong side up.

Fig. 5–16. Finished lid. Note unsewn side for attaching to the box.

**3.** Layer one lining square and the box lid square, right sides together. Place these two pieces on top of the second lining piece (fig. 5–15). It doesn't matter whether the second lining is right side up or not. Baste the layers, then trim the lid to 9½" square. Stitch the lid pieces together along the sides and front, leaving the back edge of the lid unsewn. Turn the lid right side out through the back opening (fig. 5–16.).

**4.** Quilt the lid. Experiment with various straight quilting lines. You can use all persimmon stitch (described on page 150) or mix it with a straight running stitch. Use pearl cotton thread and a sashiko needle.

**5.** For the sides of the box, place the light and dark 3⅞" x 23¼" strips right sides together. Following figure 5–17, make 12 half-square units. Trim off the dog ears.

**6.** Sew three half-square units together for each side of the box. To attach a side piece to the 9½" box base, place the side piece on top of the base, right sides together. Start with your needle ¼" in from the edge and backstitch. Sew the seam and stop ¼" from the edge and backstitch again. Repeat for the remaining three sides. Leave the corners unstitched for now.

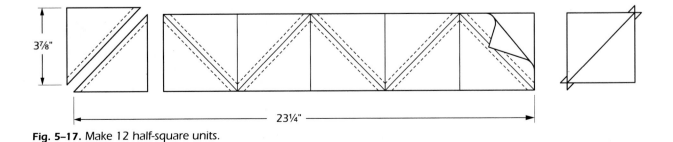

Fig. 5–17. Make 12 half-square units.

**7.** Stack the 16" box lining and the box, right sides together, on top of the 16" batting. Sew all three layers together by sewing around the side pieces, one at a time, starting and stopping ¼" from the seam and backstitching each time (fig. 5–18). Leave the area unsewn where the lid will be attached, so you can turn the box right side out after it is trimmed.

**8.** Trim all the extra batting and lining away, following the shape of the box with its sides. Clip the inside corners, then turn the box right side out through the opening. Press lightly. Baste the layers together along the edges and through the center to prepare for quilting.

**9.** With raw edges aligned and right sides together, sew the outer layers of the lid and box together. Turn under the inner raw edge of the lid and hand stitch it to the box to cover the remaining raw edges. Quilt the base and sides either by hand or machine.

*Note that I used a black pearl cotton for the sashiko and the hand quilting.*

**10.** With the box right side out, whipstitch the corners together (fig. 5–19). Sew the button on the center front side.

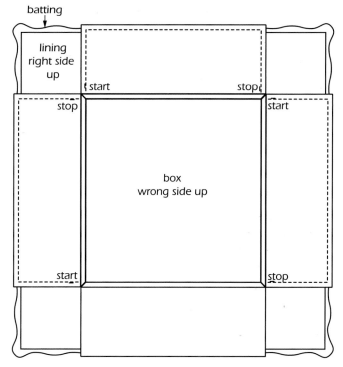

**Fig. 5–18.** Sew the three outside edges of each side piece, starting and stopping ¼" from the seam.

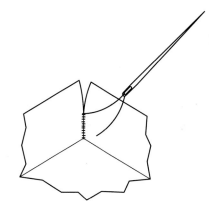

**Fig. 5–19.** Whipstitch each corner.

# Sashiko Persimmon Stitch

The persimmon stitch is formed from pairs of uneven rows alternated with pairs of even rows. In the uneven rows, the stitches alternate in checkerboard fashion. In the even rows, the stitches are aligned vertically (fig. 5–20).

The soft box lid has seven pairs of rows, for a total of 14 rows. Use the pattern on this page to lightly draw your stitching lines on the lid before layering the pieces. You may need a light source underneath the pattern for tracing it to the fabric. Repeat the pattern as needed to create as many rows as you would like.

*For any experienced quilter, instead of tracing the pattern, you can mark each horizontal row with a straight line. Then make ¼" quilting stitches along each line to create the persimmon pattern. It helps to follow the pairs of uneven rows.*

Sew all the horizontal stitches first. Then go back and stitch the vertical ones (fig. 5–21). Note how the design forms as you make the vertical stitches.

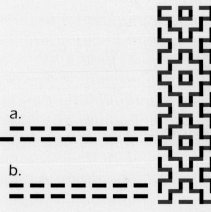
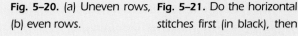

**Fig. 5–20.** (a) Uneven rows, (b) even rows.

**Fig. 5–21.** Do the horizontal stitches first (in black), then the vertical ones (in red).

Full-sized for a 9" width.

# Not Another Tote Bag

TONS OF TOTES, 86" x 86", by the author.

# Not Another Tote Bag

In every quilter's closet there lurk stacks of tote bags. Now, you can tote just so much, so it is only natural to start trimming away and thinking quilt. Random sizes lead to an even more adventurous setting and placement. This quilt contains many memories of all my travels and experiences with students.

**Finished size: 86" x 86"**

## MATERIALS

Lots of tote bags of various sizes. This quilt features 51 tote bag faces.

Border: 1¾ yards. I suggest going to a decorator store for a heavier, canvas-type fabric.

Binding: 32" square. Makes a bias-cut or straight-grain binding cut 2½" wide.

Rickrack: 8 packages of various colors with 2½ yards per package

106 Assorted buttons

Backing: 5 yards

Batting: a pre-washed flannel sheet, queen-sized

## Method

**1.** Trim away the handles, sides, and backing of each tote – save, but I am not sure for what! Working on a design surface of your choice (bed, floor, batting hung on wall), start arranging the bag faces.

*I tried to juggle colors and events. Working in vertical rows, I made seven rows. In arranging, I tried not to have the intersections align because of the bulk.*

**2.** Because of the heavier canvas fabrics, it's best not to join the totes with seams; instead, overlap the raw edges with a straight stitch.

**3.** Once the totes are secured, enhance each seam with rickrack, mixing as many colors and widths as you have available.

**4.** For the border, cut strips of fabric 6½" wide. Piece the strips together for a 96" length, four times.

**5.** Find the center of the quilt sides and the center of each border. Matching the centers, pin the borders to the quilt. Sew the borders, starting and stopping ¼" from the corners (fig. 5–22, page 153).

**6.** Overlap the corners and trim off the excess fabric, as shown in figure 5–23, page 153. Fold the corners as shown in figure 5–24, page 153, and use the 45-degree line of your rotary ruler to draw a line to the corner. Sew on that line and trim the excess fabric from the seam allowance for a perfect mitered corner.

**7.** You can use a prewashed flannel sheet for the batting. Add rickrack along the seams. Tie-tack each rickrack intersection with a button. Bind the layers.

*The button sew-on program for my sewing machine saved me time and was very efficient. Binding was completed with a wide, serpentine machine stitch.*

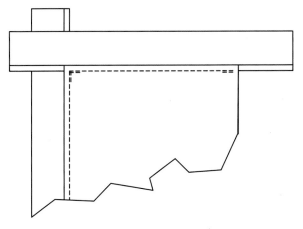

Fig. 5–22. When attaching the borders, be sure to stop and start ¼" from the corners.

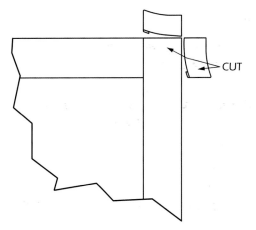

Fig. 5–23. Overlap the corners and cut off the excess fabric.

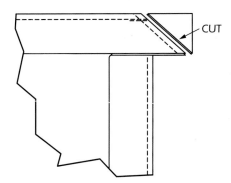

Fig. 5–24. Sew on the 45-degree line, then trim, leaving a ¼" seam allowance.

# Conclusion

## *Everything has a season and so does quilting.*

**M**y association with lap quilting has continued for more than thirty years. Today, most of my quilts are made as whole quilt tops, which are quilted in my lap, one area at a time. It was my sectional, quilt-as-you-go quilting that was the springboard for my television shows. It allowed many people to make that initial start in quiltmaking. The freedom of lap quilting in blocks or rows adapts well to either machine or hand quilting. There is something about watching someone else do a task, either in a classroom or on television, that makes it seem more feasible. Soon, you are saying, "I can do that myself." Nothing thrills me more than sharing ideas and watching the growing confidence of someone learning a new quilt pattern. The "beyond" part of my Freedom Escape retreats are reflected in two other week-long workshops at the John C. Campbell Folk School in Brasstown, North Carolina, and at The Nine Quarter Circle Ranch in Gallatin Gateway, Montana. At these venues, the concentrated efforts and the personalized guidance result in great success. These places nurture friendly competition as one tries to out-stitch the next quilter.

Early in my teaching days, I received a lovely letter from a surgeon's wife, telling me how her husband's eyes sparkled and he stopped short when he saw me draw a knot down the length of the thread. He implants pacemakers. It's not just quiltmakers who benefit from knowing about quilting.

Everything has a season and so does quilting. Over the years, I have watched the trends and new ideas all furthered by books, fabrics, notions, magazines, Web sites, conventions, and television shows. This exposure has enabled quilting to thrive and grow as an art medium and as a utilitarian necessity in the home. I hope you have enjoyed these patterns, many of which have been previewed on my television shows. Take some time and document your quilt legacy. You will find fun times and joy in all of your stitches.

# Quilters' Alphabet

**Q**uilters have their own language. There are definitions that explain our craft and how we make quilts. You can study this dictionary to understand our techniques.

**Appliqué** Cut-out figures sewn to a larger foundation piece of fabric. The application can be made several ways: basted under raw edges or needle-turned raw edges secured with a hidden slip stitch, buttonhole stitching on raw edges, machine satin stitching, or blind hem machine stitching.

**Backing** The bottom or back layer of a quilt, often called the "lining." Avoid taffeta or slippery backing fabrics and percale sheets. Preshrinking is advised. Create two or more seams when joining fabric, rather than a centered seam. Today, multi-colored backings are acceptable. For lap quilting, print backing fabric helps to disguise the connecting seams.

**Baste** A temporary running stitch used to secure fabric before machine stitching or hand quilting. Keep knots visible and use a contrasting thread. Start in the center and work outward, basting about every 6" to 7" for a large quilt.

**Batting** The filler or middle part of the quilt sandwich, which becomes the insulation. Batting comes in various forms: polyester, cotton, wool, and blends.

**Bias** The true diagonal of a fabric, which has more give and stretch. You can find the bias by folding the lengthwise straight of grain at an exact 45-degree angle to the crosswise threads. Bias is often used as binding for a quilt.

**Binding** A narrow strip of folded fabric sewn to the outside raw edges of a quilt. Binding is prepared either on the straight of grain or the bias.

**Biscuit quilting** A puff type of quilt made by stuffing batting or even nylon hose into a pocket created when a square of fabric is sewn to a smaller foundation square. There should be 1" difference between the top square and the bottom square, with a pleat centered on each side. The stuffed squares are sewn in rows, with a backing tie-tacked to the puff panels.

**Block** A unit of patchwork or appliqué, usually in a square form, which is repeated to construct the quilt top.

**Borders** Panels that frame and set off a block or an entire quilt. The corners may be mitered or squared off. A contrasting square or block is sometimes set in each corner. Borders may have appliquéd accents or pieced insets.

**Cathedral Window quilt** A coverlet of layered material with scrap fabric squares, the windows, which are inserted into folded muslin squares. It is sometimes referred to as the "year quilt." It has neither batting nor quilting.

**Catywhompus** When the top and bottom layers of a quilt shift or become askew, we say that things are catywhompus, or that catywhompus has happened.

**Comforter** A bedcover stuffed with polyester or down, usually machine or factory stitched in a decorator or satin fabric.

**Crosshatch** Diagonal or right-angle straight lines created on the quilt top as a guide for hand or machine quilting.

**Crazy Patch** A form of patchwork in which odd shapes of fabric come together, either cut from templates or attached free-form to a foundation fabric. Embroidery stitches accent the seam lines.

**Dangling threads** In lap quilting (once blocks or rows have been connected), a quilting line left unfinished where the needle has been removed to be rethreaded.

**Dog ears** Triangular extensions formed when diagonal pieces are sewn together. These should be snipped off or "pruned" to relieve pieced sections of extra bulk.

**Echo quilting** Multiple, evenly spaced quilting lines that outline a pieced or appliquéd shape and move outward like ripples in a lake.

# Quilters' Alphabet

**English piecing** Patchwork piecing achieved by hand basting fabric pieces, cut with a turn-under allowance, onto cut-out template shapes. The basted pieces are held right sides together and joined by whipstitching.

**Embroidery floss** Cotton, rayon, or silk floss used as decoration on appliqué and crazy-patch blocks, usually done with three strands of floss and an embroidery needle.

**Fabric** The prime necessity in all quiltmaking. "fabric" comprises the pieced, whole-cloth, or appliquéd top, and the backing. Cotton proves to be the best. Avoid tightly woven fabrics, such as percale sheets. Likewise, loosely woven or gauze-like fabrics can allow the batting to penetrate. Thick fabrics interfere with the joining of seams because of the extra bulk, and nappy fabrics hide the quilting stitches.

**Flexicurve** A flexible rubber ruler used in forming curved patchwork. It is sometimes called a "memory curve" because it retains its shape until it is reshaped.

**Foolproof knot** A tidy, dependable knot made by wrapping a single thread around the needle, somewhat like the beginning of a French knot, and then sliding the wraps down the thread length. It replaces the finger twirl we used to make in home sewing.

**Friendship quilt** Sometimes referred to as an Album or autograph quilt. It is a special quilt completed as a group effort, incorporating either different themes or using the same block throughout.

**Fudging** Making things work when they are not quite perfect. In patchwork, fudging usually refers to manipulating fabrics to make intersections fit together.

**Grain line** The direction of the weave or construction of the yarns in fabric. The warp yarns run parallel to the selvage, while the woof (also known as weft) yarns form the right angle, interlacing to make the fabric. The weft is also known as the crosswise grain. Any line on the fabric that is not parallel to either of these is off grain.

**Half-square triangle** A right-angle triangle. When two half-square triangles of equal size are joined on their long, bias edges, a square is formed.

**In the ditch** Quilting along a seam on the side opposite the seam allowances.

**Lap quilting** To quilt small areas of layered materials in one's lap, with or without a frame. A whole basted quilt can be quilted in small sections, or small, separate sections can be quilted and later joined into a quilt top.

**Marking** The process of transferring designs onto a quilt top in order to have a line to follow when quilting. Various methods can be used: fabric marker, water-soluble pen (test on fabric first), thin sliver of worn soap, contact paper cut in special shapes, masking tape, or a chalk roller. The goal is for the hand quilting to be seen and the marking line to disappear.

**Masterpiece quilt** An exceptionally fine quilt made to display the best of quilting, piecework, or appliqué. A quilt executed with the best of fabrics, more difficult curves, tiny piecework, or intricate appliqué, and quilted in a good light with total concentration.

**Meandering** A quilting term referring to squiggly puzzle-like lines created either by hand or machine. A small, finely worked meandering line is called "stipple quilting."

**Medallion quilt** A quilt top focused on a central square, diamond, or other motif, with multiple borders or designs expanding outward.

**Mitering** A 45-degree diagonal seam at the corner of a block, block frame, or border.

**Notions** Paraphernalia necessary to quiltmaking, such as thread, needles, scissors, thimbles, etc.

**Off hand** The hand that rests under the quilt, guiding the needle and feeling that all three layers have been caught in the process.

**On point** A block-rotated 45 degrees, so that it looks like a diamond shape, is said to be set on point.

**Patchwork** The art of building a large piece of decorative cloth from smaller pieces. Should possibly be renamed "patchfun."

**Piecing or piecework** The process of sewing two or more pieces of fabric together. Piecing can be done on the sewing machine or by hand, with a regular length stitch, coordinating thread, and a ¼" seam allowance. There are special sewing machine feet that help the sewer gauge a ¼" allowance.

**Prune** To trim away excess fabric or triangular points to even the edges of a block.

**Quarter-square triangle** When a square is divided on both diagonals, each of the four resulting right-angle triangles is called a "quarter-square triangle."

**Quilt** Any bedcover with three layers comprised of the decorative top, filling, and backing. These layers are secured with a running stitch referred to as quilting lines.

**Reverse appliqué** A method of appliqué in which two or more layers of cloth are sewn together and top layers are cut through, revealing the underneath layers. This technique is exemplified by mola fabrics, made by Panamanian Indians.

**Sampler quilts** A quilt comprised of various blocks made by using different techniques and designs. These blocks may be the same size or unequal size.

**Sashings** Strips of fabric sewn between blocks, sometimes called "lattice stripping."

**Setting** The relationship of one block to the next in an arrangement to form a whole quilt top. "Setting squares" refers to the fabric squares at the intersections of sashing strips.

**Stencil** Designs on paper or plastic that are transferred to a quilt top to provide guide lines for quilting.

**String quilts** Regular or irregular strips of fabric secured to a foundation to create a quilt top.

**Template** A pattern made from durable material (cardboard, plastic, sandpaper, soft vinyl, gridded freezer paper) and used to transfer shapes onto fabric. Templates are a key factor in precision piecework, ensuring uniformity in the size and shape of the pieces.

**Thread** A fine string of a fibrous material made of filaments twisted together. The "glue" of all quilts.

**Tied quilt** Quilt top, filler, and backing fastened together with yarn or thick thread at regular intervals.

**Throw** An Afghan-sized quilt used to cover a small area.

**Toile** Pastoral scenes printed on fabric, often in one color on a light background.

**Trapunto** A softly sculptured effect, created during the quilting process, by stuffing a pattern from the backside, giving it more dimensions. Mock trapunto is achieved by adding extra batting in the middle part under a certain area to be elevated.

**Unstitch** To rip out.

**Vest** A sleeveless upper-body, garment. Quilters quite often decorate vests with patchwork or appliqué. In Europe, a vest is called a "waistcoat."

**Wadding** The European term for batting.

**Whole-cloth quilt** A quilt of one continuous fabric (no piecing or appliqué) with an overall quilting design.

**Yo-yo** A small, gathered, circular fabric piece. Several yo-yos can be whipstitched together for decoration.

# Resources

**International Quilt Association**
7660 Woodway, Suite 550
Houston, TX 77063
www.quilts.com

**Acoustic Neuroma Association**
600 Peachtree Parkway, Suite #108
Cumming, GA 30041
www.ANAUSA.org

**Learning Resources** (plastic blocks)
380 N Fairway Drive
Vernon Hills, IL 60061
www.learningresources.com
Also, www.georgiabonesteel.com

**The Blue Ridge School of Photography**
E-mail: brsp@loganphotographics.com

**Freedom Escape**
Contact: Lee Roskamp Lundahl
2278 Kings Pointe Dr., Largo, FL 33774

**Edward Larson**
821 Canyon Road
Santa Fe, NM 87501
E-mail: edsart@cybermesa.com

**My Quilt Shoppe**, in Flat Rock, NC
www.MyQuiltShoppe.com

For about 20 years the author owned and operated Bonesteel Hardware & Quilt Corner. They are no longer in business, but she is associated with My Quilt Shoppe.

For notion availability, such as Grid Grip™, plastic blocks or silk handbag kits, see:
www.georgiabonesteel.com

# About the Author

What began as a hobby for Georgia Bonesteel has developed into a highly visible career for more than 30 years. She is perhaps best known for her role in bringing her art into the homes of people across the country through *Lap Quilting*, produced by The Center of North Carolina Public TV, seen on many television stations. Her goal has been to refine the traditional methods to provide a quicker and easier way to make quilts, without sacrificing quality.

Teaching, lecturing, and quiltmaking make a full-time occupation for Georgia. She has recently been honored with the International Quilt Association's Silver Star Salute in 2000, the Bernina® of America 2002 Leadership Award and induction into the Hall of Fame in 2003. Now with her ninth book, *Georgia Bonesteel's Quiltmaking Legacy*, she presents a bounty of new quilts and exciting projects highlighted with stories from her colorful quilt life on the road.

# Other AQS Books

#6516          us$21.95

#6414          us$25.95

#6204          us$19.95

#6408          us$22.95

#6517          us$21.95

#6000          us$24.95

#6293          us$24.95

#6298          us$24.95

#6009          us$19.95